SLEEPING BETWEEN GIANTS
BOOK II

DAVE JAFFE

ALSO BY DAVE JAFFE

Sleeping between Giants

Life, If You Could Call It That, With A Terrier

Book I

Budleigh, the Early Year

PRAISE FOR
SLEEPING BETWEEN GIANTS BOOKS

"In 'Sleeping Between Giants Book II, Ask a Terrier,' Dave Jaffe's wisecracking dog Budleigh dispenses hilarious advice to both canines and Giants (aka humans) who have no clue about things canine (or even human). Budleigh is the Dear Abby of pooches. Or maybe Dear Abby is the Budleigh of advice columnists. At any rate, this compilation of letters and answers will have you — that's right — howling. It's as funny a book as you will find and even more fun than a chew toy. Read it to your dog, who will love Budleigh. So, clueless Giant, will you."

— Jerry Zezima, nationally syndicated humorist and bestselling author

"People put great stock in getting information straight from "the horse's mouth," but award winner Dave Jaffe's latest book 'Sleeping between Giants Book II, Ask a Terrier' proves getting it straight from the dog's mouth is infinitely more fun, if not particularly accurate. Budleigh dispenses advice with the unfailing confidence and boldness of a true terrier. Jaffe may have done the transcribing—exploiting his unfair advantage of opposable thumbs—but, make no mistake, the wise and hilarious words are all Budleigh's. Four paws up and a big tail wag for this sure hit.

— Lee Gaitan, award-winning author of "My Pineapples Went to Houston" and "Lite Whines and Laughter"

"When I tell you that [Sleeping Between Giants, Book I: Life, If You Could Call It That, With A Terrier] by Dave Jaffe is a funny book, you seriously have to believe me. I had to stop reading it in public because I was making a spectacle of myself, laughing, snorting, and insisting that my husband quit doing what he was doing so that he could read the passage I was laughing at."

— *Lori Duff, author of Amazon #1 bestseller, "You Know I Love You Because You're Still Alive."*

"[Sleeping Between Giants, Book I] will keep you wide awake laughing uproariously! Author Dave Jaffe chronicles life with his quirky rescue terrier with more hilarious quips than the number of pellets in a ginormous bag of kibble. We get comedy (and some seriousness) about Budleigh and his older 'co-dog' Brisby – their baths, the chewing on things not to be chewed, the on-leash or off-leash question, doggie costumes, and veterinarian stuff. (One line invokes the age-old question: 'Why don't Giants ever have to wear cones?') There's even a bit of political commentary … also funny photos and funny comic strips from Jaffe, the gifted humorist/multi-award-winning blogger."

— *Dave Astor, author of "Fascinating Facts About Famous Fiction Authors"*

Sleeping between Giants
Book II

Ask a Terrier

Professional Advice from a Licensed Dog

Dave Jaffe

GRAY-GRAY
PUBLISHING

Sleeping between Giants, Book II
Ask a Terrier: Professional Advice from a Licensed Dog
Published by Cray-Cray Publishing
Address inquiries to:
Cray-Cray Publishing
P.O. Box 7065
Deerfield, IL 60015
CrayCrayPublishing@gmail.com

Cover by Tatiana Vila, Vila Design.

Print ISBN: 978-1-7341925-2-0
Ebook ISBN: 978-1-7341925-3-7

First Edition.

Thank you for respecting the hard work of this author who is weak from hunger, infirm with age, and lacking in friends.

For information about special discounts available for bulk purchases, sales promotions, fund-raising, book clubs, speaking engagements, and educational needs, Contact Donna Cavanagh, www.HumorOutcasts.com or dtcav@aol.com.

Visit Dave Jaffe at his website,
www.SleepingBetweenGiants.com.
Contact: dave@SleepingBetweenGiants.com

Dedication

*To Denise
and the four,
plus one.*

CONTENTS

Introduction: From Rags to Riches ...
Or At Least Chew Toys 1

Budleigh! (-udleigh-udleigh...) In! (-iin-iin...) Space!
(-ace-ace...)..4

The Truth Ain't Out There!..8

Talkin' TED 13

Wake Up and Smell the COVID!... 17

Unmasking the Mask.. 22

Why? What Are You? 25

Paper Training.. 27

Don't Hold the Phone... 32

Zooming Isn't Like Running.. 37

Sheltering Outside the Shelter.. 42

Is It a Terrier World? Is It?.. 47

Budleigh Analyzes Therapy 49

Can't We All Just Get Along? 52

Mark of the Hallmark.. 55

It's In the Bag! 60

Oh, Great ... Another New Collar.. 64

Budleigh Addresses a Royal Pain 67

How the Dogs Are Voting..72

Just How Infra Is Our Structure?.................................76

Semper Canis! 79

What's Bugging Budleigh?...83

Destroy All Monsters!..86

Not a Black Hole Lot of Excitement for Dogs.............89

Does Anybody Really Know What Time It Is?.............92

Budleigh Goes All Scatolog-ICK-al! 95

Budleigh Takes a Walk on the Wild Side 99

Cloning Has Budleigh Seeing Double 102

What is "Dog" Backwards, Again? 106

Dogs and Children – When Species Collide 108

Your Dog or Your Boyfriend.
Is That Really a Question?.. 112

Budleigh Reminds Vacationers,
"Hey, Ya Got This Dog Here!"..................................... 115

Dogs Are a Bargain! Except For the Money.............. 119

Budleigh Offers Food for Thought............................. 123

Hero or Hungry? 127

The Latest Dirt on Dog Germs................................... 130

Winnin' and Waggin'!... 133

The Giant as Emoticon 135

Washing Machines of Mass Destruction............................. 138

The Veterinarian is In!
Budleigh Offers Advice on Not Swallowing Pills.............. 141

Extolling Consoling... 145

The Dogs Strip: (Not as Dirty as it Sounds!) 149

EpiDogue.. 157

Acknowledgments.. 159

Haven't had enough of Budleigh?
Try living with him!... 161

Praise for Sleeping between Giants, Book I 163

INTRODUCTION

FROM RAGS TO RICHES …
OR AT LEAST CHEW TOYS

Dogs have much to teach us about life besides the best spots to poop.

As a fully qualified terrier, Budleigh is devoted to sorting out the lives of his readers in much the way he sorts out the lives of rabbits or other small prey.

In **Sleeping between Giants, Book I: Budleigh, The Early Year**, we were introduced to a young terrier I met in a shelter after his arrest by police in Waukegan, Illinois, on charges of vagrancy, loitering, and panhandling, which were false, and of being a homeless dog, which was true.

Technically.

Designated as "Bandit" by the shelter staff, who usually added a scornful "Hmph!," this terrier was released of his own recognizance into my care after I posted a $50 bond, plus vaccinations.

On the drive home I explained that he was welcome in our home and that we intended to change his name to Budleigh for personal reasons too complex to explain until Sleeping between Giants, Book III. Budleigh eagerly took on this new title, rejecting "Bandit", his biker gang name.

Like many formerly incarcerated canines, Budleigh acclimated quickly to life on the outside, now spent primarily inside. He formed a deep and trustful friendship with Brisby, our older dog, a Schnoodle who would serve as confidant and parole officer.

While not a superior intellect, Brisby believed in playing by the rules, provided those rules were never more complicated than, "Give me your paw!" He tutored Budleigh in all the life lessons he'd acquired in his nine years. Budleigh mastered them by dinner time.

Cunning, intelligent, and fleetingly thoughtful, Budleigh was proof of those old adages, "Smart as a Terrier" and "Did he break the skin?" Determined never to return to life on the streets, Budleigh committed himself to raising up downtrodden dogs and their confused Giants on the wings of his fur.

"I was a shelter dog, you know.
Sooo … can I have your toast?"

Part teacher, part preacher, but mostly … ya know … a dog, Budleigh began sharing what he used in place of actual wisdom; first with neighborhood canines, then later with the small not-for-profit packs that ran around the local dog parks. His razor-sharp mind and keen wit belied his rough exterior; that roughness due to his thick, wiry undercoat.

What began as a small offering of unwanted counsel has grown into an empire of sketchy advice with Budleigh as Supreme Misguider. His internet column, Ask a Terrier, has been translated into numerous languages, none of which he understands. Fans of Budleigh's speaking tours – mostly dogs – stand in line for hours howling for tickets. Or maybe just howling at each other.

Hard to say.

The popularity of Budleigh's column, Ask a Terrier: Professional Advice from a Licensed Dog, led to this book, coincidentally titled Ask a Terrier: Professional Advice from a Licensed Dog. This compendium gathers letters from dogs and Giants on a wide range of topics; some touching, some tender, but none in a foreign language that Budleigh understands. Budleigh's wry, amusing, and sometimes hilarious opinions will have you howling with laughter. Or maybe just howling at each other.

Hard to say …

BUDLEIGH! (-UDLEIGH-UDLEIGH…) IN! (-IIN-IIN…) SPACE! (-ACE-ACE…)

Dear Budleigh,

In these disturbing times of political turmoil, pandemic risk, and economic uncertainty, what a warming comfort it is to know that billionaires can joyride in space. Imagine my delight at the historic space flights of Jeff Bezos and Richard Branson … excuse me. Sir Richard Branson. Of course, I didn't actually witness these events since I was stuck in traffic in my nine-year-old Prius, slowly inching my way to my crap, low-wage job.

In case you can't tell, Budleigh, I'm being sarcastic. I think it's unfair that outer space is just for the wealthy. Do you agree?

Please share your down-to-Earth wisdom with us. (See what I did there? With that pun there? I just made that up!)

Be well!

A real smart-ass in Seattle

Dear Smart-ass,

You might not enjoy hearing this, but I cannot rail against billionaires as I am one.

4

Apparently, this advice column business pays rather well, I'm told by my unpaid intern *Per Se* who handles all my finances. I find "money" quite confusing, so at *Per Se's* urging, I assigned to him control of my assets, investments, and savings. He says he'll only alert me if funds run so low that I can't afford new tug-tug toys. *Per Se* insists that I've a million billion "moneys," which is like 10 in dog years, so I've no worries.

I mention this because despite my enormous wealth, I was denied a berth on the historic flights of both Jeff and *Sir*.

While I'm grateful that these two risked their lives to prove galactic travel safe for Canines, I resent that they pooled their tremendous resources to bar me from outer space. It speaks to the very worst species-ism! Maybe even voter intimidation.

"Four small steps for a Dog ..."

But the preponderance of blame falls on the National Aeronautics and Space Administration or NASA. (*Professional credo:* "Whatever you say, Mr. Bezos!")

This federal agency requires all potential "astronauts" to submit an extensive "questionnaire" about their "health" and "fitness" for such conditions as "gravitational acceleration" and "G-force." Oh, and whether they're a "dog."

Seriously? C'mon, this isn't rocket science!

Among the impertinent and intrusive questions in this survey:

How tall are you? (NASA height requirements are between 5 ft. 2 in. and 6 ft. 3 in.)

Obviously, this is a trick question to weed out the four-legged and the measurement-challenged. I happen to be the ideal height for my weight. So, I had *Per Se* fill in, "Scruffy black with white markings."

Spatial reasoning: In the pictured three-dimensional shape, predict the color of the unseen face.

Again, tricky. My response, "Grey! Just not as grey as the rest of the grey."

Number sequencing: Find the next number in this sequence – 1, 2, 6, 21, 88.

Played it safe here! Pretty sure we're talking about "moneys" again. My answer: "Scruffy black with white markings."

General knowledge: What is the correct order of the planets moving out from the sun?

Street sign. Hydrant. Brown grassy patch. Garbage can. (They *never* put that away!) Something grey. Something *bigger* and grey. Street sign. (Maybe the same one.)

Do you get motion sickness?

Only when I dig up and eat too many motions.

And for this, I was turned down for space travel? Very well, Jeff and *Sir!* You'll be hearing from my unpaid intern shortly.

Budleigh

THE TRUTH AIN'T OUT THERE!

Howdy, Budleigh!

So, like, UFOs? Does this new Pentagon declassified report on unidentified flying objects reveal any threats to Dillie, my Greyhound? I've watched "Alien" like a dozen times, so you can be straight with me. Is Dillie in danger?

Oh, and Humanity?

Eyes on the Skies in Michigan. And Dillie!

Dear Eyes and Dillie,

I was eager to scrutinize this long-anticipated, highly technical report on Unidentified Aerial Phenomena. My initial impressions were that it was written on paper that shredded easily, but was *very* chewy.

For a deeper dive, I had my unpaid intern *Per Se* actually *read* the nine-page report, which he did with a speed and professionalism borne of having thumbs. In his PowerPoint, *Per Se* outlined the report's conclusions: the U.S. government doesn't know what these UFOs are or if they're extraterrestrial.

Also, why the report is so chewy.

Such dubious results will disappoint UFO and alien spacecraft enthusiasts, many of whom consider "Independence Day" a documentary.

"In a universe so big, so grand," they ask, "why couldn't other intelligent life exist? Also, where's the remote and are we out of Doritos?"

All reasonable questions. Yet, so typically Giant-centric! They fail to focus on the main issue. If it's difficult for Giants to identify objects in the sky, what with all their Science and PowerPoints and chewy paper, imagine how much more baffling for Canines. We barely recognize the stuff we eat off the floor.

Do dogs believe in UFOs? The question is, do UFOs believe in dogs?

Investigators were unable to explain more than 140 cases of Unidentified Flying Objects (*acronym: "UFO"*) or Unidentified Aerial Phenomena (*acronym: also "UFO"*). Yet many encounters were reported by Naval aviators who have excellent vision, although a sadly inferior sense of smell.

While the report has created a stir among Giants, in dog parks across the nation Canines are abuzz with speculative concern:

GERMAN SCHNAUZER: "Look! I'm just saying that if they're not aliens and they're not foreign military, how do we *know* they're not squirrels?"

PUG: "Squirrels climb trees. They can't fly. Can they?"

GERMAN SCHNAUZER: "Who knows what they're doing up there!"

CHOCOLATE LABRADOR: "I've heard they store stuff. And that they're nuts!"

PUG: "No, no, no! They *store … nuts!* That's all one thing."

BERNESE MOUNTAIN DOG: "You know where I'd store 'em? Caves! Say, guess where you find caves!"

PUG: "We are *not* going there!"

BERNESE MOUNTAIN DOG: (*Snarling*) "Your face is squished! And your coat is rough! Everybody says so."

BUDLEIGH: "Stay focused, everyone. We're discussing UFOs. Has anyone actually *seen* one?"

Much head turning and ear scratching. Bernese Mountain Dog leaps to feet.

BUDLEIGH: "—that wasn't in a cave?"

Bernese Mountain Dog lies down, dejected.

BUDLEIGH: "C'mon, guys! Any sightings of the weird? The inexplicable? The eerie?"

GOLDEN RETRIEVER: "Well ... there was that van that took Roxy the Boxer."

PUG: "Who?"

GOLDEN RETRIEVER: "Before your time. Roxy had ... issues."

PIT BULL: "*Society* had the issues!"

PUG: "What sort of issues?"

GOLDEN RETRIEVER: "He could be ... argumentative."

PUG: "With dogs?"

GOLDEN RETRIEVER: "Dogs, yes ... yes..."

CHOCOLATE LAB: "—and Giants!"

STANDARD POODLE: "—also children!"

YORKSHIRE TERRIER: "—ice cream truck drivers!"

YELLOW LAB: "—anyone wearing yellow."

DALMATIAN: "Or patterns."

SHAR-PEI: "—wrinkles."

ROTTWEILER: "—loud, piercing sounds and flashing lights."

GOLDEN RETRIEVER: "One day, Roxy got in a disagreement with some schoolchildren. Actually, a busload of children."

BEAGLE: "—then a firefighter."

DALMATIAN: "—and several police officers."

YORKSHIRE TERRIER: "—from nearby towns."

GOLDEN RETRIEVER: "That's when a strange, featureless van appeared. And Roxy was mysteriously transported inside."

ROTTWEILER: "More like forced. With ropes."

GOLDEN RETRIEVER: "Then the doors closed and the vehicle zoomed away silently into the darkness."

PIT BULL: "Well, except for the loud, piercing siren and flashing lights."

ROTTWEILER "Yikes! Roxy wouldn't have liked *that!*"

PUG: "Where did Roxy go?"

GOLDEN RETRIEVER: "Probably back to his home world."

ROTTWEILER: "Or to a really, *really* nice farm!"

Budleigh

Talkin' TED

A question for you, Budleigh.

Have you considered giving a TED Talk? You've such an essential grasp of the issues and themes that trouble us all. Well, mostly dogs. But although I'm a Giant, I've also picked up many useful tips from you. And frankly, you've more valuable advice to share than most TED talkers who drone on about saving the environment, or technology that solves world hunger, or extending life through emotional fulfilment. Yawn! We all just want to know the best tug-tug toys.

Well, mostly dogs.

As a loyal reader, I urge you to expand your forum to the TED stage. The world would benefit. Plus, you'd look so adorable wearing one of those headset microphones!

Hoping to Manage Your Career,

Greg P., Buffalo, NY

Dear Greg,

I've thought about giving a TED Talk. Especially in advance of the release of my self-help book, "How to Be Less Whatever It Is *You* Are and More *Me*." But while I lecture extensively, and often to groups that are feral, TED might not be my ideal forum.

13

This is based on research by my intern, *Per Se*, who I assigned to investigate TED Talk requirements instead of his usual job separating Kibbles from Bits.

Look, I'm not a diva. The Bits are delicious, the Kibbles merely decorative.

Shockingly, TED speakers are required to follow – you'll pardon the expression – rules. *Rules!* That's *so* Giant. As a Terrier, skirting rules is my *raison d'être* (French for "My teeth were here first!") Imagine a world where everyone follows rules. Chaos! No, the opposite: Well-behaved! That's worse.

A popular TED Talk can establish a dog as a thought leader. And a Good Boy!

Consider the rule that a TED Talk run no longer than 18 minutes. Is that 18 Giant or Dog minutes? Regardless of the Canine Conversion Rate – which is something like one Giant year equals a furlong – I've a problem. When I speak to groups of animals, I tell them everything in two minutes. Then I repeat it because they weren't listening. Add another minute for snarls – mine and the audience's. Then autograph, autograph, autograph! Hand me the check. I'm outta there.

But a full 18-minute talk? That's gonna cost a *lot* more Kibbles 'n Bits.

Well, Bits.

Other provisos *Per Se* found: TED Talkers should present the next big idea, have no political or religious agenda, and pitch no products or services from the stage. Outraged at these demands, I sought input from my fellow lecturers at the dog park before firing *Per Se*.

LABRADOR RETRIEVER: "Is retrieving a big idea? Or do I have to retrieve something … ya know … *big?*"

BERNESE MOUNTAIN DOG: (*Breathless*) "Like a mountain? I've a PowerPoint!"

IRISH WOLFHOUND: "Look, I'm not Irish. I've never seen a wolf. I've nothing to talk about. There's been a terrible mistake!"

BUDLEIGH: "You don't have to TED Talk."

IRISH WOLFHOUND: "They won't ship me to a farm in the country?"

DACHSHUND: "Is digging a religious agenda? There's *something* under the porch stoop. No one believes me. We need to prepare!"

BUDLEIGH: "OK, you're a little scary …"

CAIRN TERRIER: "I've smelled it, too! Only it's behind the trellis in my Giants' garden. Well, what's left of their garden. They didn't believe me either."

BEAGLE: "It's hiding in the garbage can! All the garbage cans everywhere! We've got to get Giants to listen!"

PUG: "After we nose through the garbage!"

BUDLEIGH: "Settle down, everyone. A TED Talk like that will only panic the Giants. Maybe get us shipped to a farm in the country."

BERNESE MOUNTAIN DOG: "But I've a *PowerPoint!*"

BUDLEIGH: "A successful TED Talk comes from the soul."

PUG: "What's a 'soul'?"

DACHSHUND: "It's that thing under the porch stoop!"

LABRADOR RETRIEVER: "Where do we start?"

BUDLEIGH: "By being open, honest, and asking yourself this: How adorable would I be wearing one of those headset microphones?'"

Budleigh

WAKE UP AND SMELL THE COVID!

Dear Budleigh,

Am I to understand that dogs are being trained to sniff out COVID-19? Has anyone explained this to the dogs? While there is no evidence that dogs can catch and spread the virus, this begs the question: Is there evidence that dogs can catch and spread the virus?

How far along is this research? Who's conducting it? Are the brave trainees being rewarded with more than a click and a treat? Maybe a steak sandwich?

Please post your thoughts soon. Better yet, call me, since I try not to touch the computer keyboard. Or anything else.

Be well,

Jason in the Basement Behind the Furnace Under a Plastic Tarp

Dear J. BBFUPT,

You're referring, I'm sure, to the recent pilot study at the University of Helsinki in which Finnish scientists are deploying a randomized, double-blind study to determine if Canines can scent a specific olfactory signature of the novel coronavirus in the effluvium of test subjects' secretions.

Like many of my readers, I was unclear on a couple of these concepts, such as Helsinki, Finnish, deploy, randomized, double-blind, scent, olfactory, novel, effluvium, test subjects, secretions, and BBFUPT.

However, my unpaid college intern *Per Se* is majoring in reading with a minor in several interesting numbers. To explain this study, he prepared a concise, professional presentation using hand puppets, some of which I chewed up because, sadly, they contained squeakers.

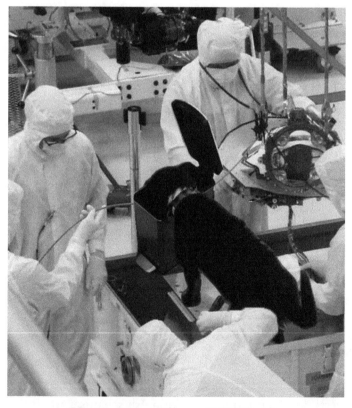

**Learning to sniff out COVID-19,
many trainee dogs insist on following their own protocols.**

As I understand it, certain diseases in Giants present a specific olfactory signature (SQUEAK-y!)…a specific olfactory signature that trained dogs (SQUEAK-y! Squeak-SQUEAK-y!)…trained dogs can sniff out with amazing accuracy.

SQUEAK-y!

Canines' ability to smell is millions of times better than Giants. Some diseases present certain volatile organic compounds. Trained dogs can detect those subtle VOCs in patients' blood, saliva, and urine.

These are a few of my favorite things!

The Finnish study indicates that COVID-19 might also give off VOCs that can be detected by dogs trained as medical diagnostic assistants, yet denied those cool white lab coats. With little difficulty, trainee dogs were able to distinguish between urine samples from COVID-19 patients and healthy subjects.

No surprise here. We're *very* practiced with the pee.

Scientists worldwide are furthering these tests by deploying their own randomized, double-blind studies—a process by which trainee dogs are blindfolded, researchers are blindfolded, then they all stumble around the laboratory bumping into expensive equipment and breaking glassware until Science happens!

To hasten results, I conducted my own field tests. In an actual field, that being the dog park.

BUDLEIGH: "OK, everyone! Take a last drink at the water bowl, then bring your sticks and tennis balls over here so we can get started."

BRISBY THE SCHNOODLE *(Budleigh's co-dog)*: "I know him! Hi, Budleigh!"

BUDLEIGH: "We've a guest lecturer today who'll be discussing how he trained to smell the pandemic."

BRISBY: "You go, Budleigh! *(Whispers excitedly)* Budleigh's my roomie!"

BUDLEIGH: "From the University of Helsinki, let me introduce … Bleu. Did I pronounce that right? 'Bleu?'"

BLOODHOUND: "Just 'Blue.'"

BUDLEIGH: "Let's give Blue a warm dog park welcome!"

(Barks, howls, some tennis balls shaking.)

BLOODHOUND: "Thank you! So, I get to smell pee. Sometimes the Science Giant gives me a cookie. I'll take questions now."

CAIRN TERRIER: "I thought your name was COVID."

BLOODHOUND: "No, it's Blue. COVID is the pandemic."

CAIRN TERRIER: "So you're not 19?"

BLOODHOUND: "I'm two."

CAIRN TERRIER: *(Muttering)* "I've gotta read the brochures better."

GREYHOUND: "Where do you keep Helsinki? Can I run there?"

BLOODHOUND: "Well, I was in a box the whole way here. But I think it's pretty far."

GREYHOUND: "OK! Never mind." *(Curls up, falls asleep.)*

GOLDEN RETRIEVER: "I'm a Retriever. I retrieve. Do you bleed?"

BLOODHOUND: "No, I smell. Professionally."

BRITISH BULLDOG: "So, this COVID? Bet it smells like chicken!"

PORTUGUESE WATER DOG: "You say *everything* smells like chicken."

BRITISH BULLDOG: "And you drink too much water! That can't be healthy."

PORTUGUESE WATER DOG: "What's with your face?"

BRITISH BULLDOG: "It's *supposed* to look like this! I'm British!"

PORTUGUESE WATER DOG: "Well, I'm part Portuguese, part water! Do we have a problem?"

(Barks, howls, more tennis ball shaking.)

BLOODHOUND: "If there are no more questions, can I have my check?"

Budleigh

UNMASKING THE MASK

Dear Budleigh,

I know all about coronavirus, but do we really need to be wearing face masks everywhere? I walk around the grocery store and feel like an extra in a Tarantino bank heist movie. A lot of these health guidelines seem confusing and arbitrary. Who should we believe?

The answer, of course, is Budleigh!

Mask or unmask? What's your opinion?

Safe in Seattle

Dear SS,

I never wear a mask for reasons of both style and snout. Style, because I'm averse to anything that blocks my black-and-white, charmingly uneven, Giant-delighting beard. It's what got me adopted. And keeps me in bacon bits.

Snout, because … well, sufficient lengths of fabric have yet to be found. Possibly my Giants' bed linens could serve, but years ago we negotiated an agreement. They would maintain limited control of the bed; I would be adopted and kept in bacon bits.

It should be noted, however, that dogs neither carry nor spread Covid-19, according to the latest fake news, fake science, fake economics, and fake White House administration mishandling. Which begs the question: Why are you asking a dog if *you*, a Giant, should wear a mask?

As my Yelly Giant explains in between swears, wearing a face mask in a public venue helps guard you from virus exposure. Also, your face covering shields other Giants from possible exposure from you.

How very mature, responsible, and dog pack-ish!

Yet some Giants balk at the face mask, even those printed with adorable little dog paws. They claim that wearing one treads on their Constitutional right to become deathly ill (See U.S. Supreme Court case 227; *Asbury v. Who Puked on the Carpet? Gross!*)

**Properly fitting a face mask is especially challenging
for the floppy-eared thumbless.**

But is wearing face masks a red state/blue state conflict? Or in the case of Canines, a light grey/not-quite-so-light-grey state issue?

As I recently took part in elections for Alpha at my dog park, I can say with confidence that politics have no place in this face mask debate. Even former Giant Vice President Pence knows this, having been derided for his lack of a mask when touring a medical clinic. He claimed he wanted to look those healthcare workers in the eye.

If he couldn't look them in the eye, I suspect that he was wearing the mask wrong. But that's a Giant issue.

More important than whether to wear the mask is *how* to wear it properly. That highly developed talent is all that separates Giants and Canines from the animals.

1. Loop the mask over your ears, if you can still find them under that unruly mass of out-of-control, badly-in-need-of-a-color hair.

2. Cover all parts of your face that appear to be holes.

3. Breathe normally. Inhale on even days. Exhale odd days.

4. To remove the mask, pinch the bridge of the nose with the three fingers you like least. Then lifting the mask away from your face, turn and run the other way.

5. Discard used masks or soak them overnight in a solution of equal parts bleach and Dr. Anthony Fauci.

Now rest. Repeat. Watch Netflix.

Budleigh

WHY? WHAT ARE YOU?

Hi Budleigh!

You're so cute! What are you, and are other dogs and their Giants jealous of your good looks?

Denise S., Deerfield, Illinois

Thank you, Denise S. Deerfield, Illinois,

Probably I'm a cross between Terriers, although not the *same* Terrier. I'll never know. I was a shelter dog, but I'm not bitter about that. And yes, everyone is jealous of me except the chipmunks in the Giants' garden that know only fear.

And respect!

Budleigh

Shelter dogs present complex pedigrees that can range from
confusing to downright frightening!

Paper Training

Dear Budleigh,

Are you kidding me? What is it with you dogs and paper? I leave my Labrador Retrievers Vex (nose above) and River (nose below) for an hour and come home to a Superbowl celebration. Yet, I know that their favorite team isn't even in contention.

I think that we'd all agree that Labrador Retrievers are the most intelligent Canines, are incapable of doing wrong, and deeply respect the personal space of others provided those spaces are tennis ball free. But to Vex and River, paper products such as napkins, tissues, toilet paper – especially toilet paper! – are catnip. Or the doggie equivalent of a controlled substance.

How can I regulate my pups' cravings for paper short of going 100-percent digital, which ain't gonna help in the bathroom.

Please call. Don't write a letter!

Alex and Jess, Chicago

Loyal, obedient, and truthful Labradors swear this was the work of terrorists. Possibly Dachshunds.

Dear Alex and Jess,

Let's first address that elephant in the room, which in this case is a Labrador Retriever. I've known many Labradors, frolicked with them, even sat with some on the boards of large nonprofit corporations. Some are good dogs, some Very Good Dogs. But intelligent? On a scale of one to ten, with me at the top, I'd give them a "Meh!" plus.

I say this, Alex and Jess, to put paper shredding into perspective.

All Canines do it, from the clever Border Collie down to that small tan-and-white hairless breed. You know, the drooly ones with the big paws? Oh, what are they called? Very yappy?

My point is that Giants needn't understand Canines. They need to understand paper.

Research by my talented and unpaid intern *Per Se* revealed valuable intelligence, although still not as intelligent as me and Border Collies. Canines and paper have long held an adversarial relationship, dwarfing such famous feuds as Hamilton vs. Burr, Ali vs. Frazier, and Senate Republicans vs. everyone else.

Long before the creation of paper, the ancient Egyptians wrote on parchment made from untanned animal hides. This led to the hasty exodus of dogs out of Egypt miles ahead of the ancient Israelites.

Paper was invented 2,000 years ago – or 14,000 in dog years – in China, which coincidentally is the origin country of those small tan-and-white hairless, drooly, big-pawed, yappy dogs whose breed is … oh, it's right on the tip of my tongue! So frustrating!

Made from a pulpy mix of mulberry tree bark, hemp, and rags, paper was used widely as wrapping, padding, ornaments, even money. But it took Canine ingenuity to demonstrate how great paper was to pee on.

The Chinese held papermaking a closely guarded secret, But the techniques spread to other lands as merchants traveled along the network of trade routes known as the Silk Road. Shrewd Canines trotted along beside them, although the Silk Road's slippery surface was a challenge for their paws. Especially those big-pawed, drooly yappers.

The Japanese are credited with transforming paper into high art through a technique of creasing, folding, and tearing called

Origami, (literal translation, "That looks *nothing* like a crane!") Attempts to withhold the secret of paper from Westerners failed, probably because it was held in a woefully insecure creased, folded, and torn origami vault. Soon all of Europe was failing to fold a proper crane.

Some Canines' paper shredding is more artistic than others.

For many centuries shredding paper was a pleasure reserved for wealthy and elite Canines. And even then, that paper had to be wrapped around bacon. This changed dramatically with the coming of the Industrial Age. Paper became plentiful thanks to the advent of powered machines like the steam-driven toilet paper dispenser. Now, shredding paper was within the grasp of the jaws of the Common Dog.

History is replete with profound Canine/paper encounters, as documented in Ken Burns' upcoming PBS documentary, "Spit that out! Bad Dog! Drop it! Drop!" Among revelations:

- An early draft of the U.S. Constitution shredded by Thomas Jefferson's dog, Monroe Doctrine, included two amendments specifically about surrendering to extraterrestrials.

- Michelangelo's elaborate design blueprints for the floor of the Sistine Chappel, lost to the piddle of his dog, Blue.

- Missing sheet music of the Beatles' "Revolution 1 through 8," mangled by George Harrison's Spaniel, I Buried Paul.

- Recovered from the dog bed of Fala, President Franklin D. Roosevelt's terrier, the original wording from Roosevelt's inaugural address: "The only thing we have to fear is fear itself. Oh, and the Great Depression, Prohibition, unemployment, the New Deal, the Old Deal, and surrendering to extraterrestrials."

So, Alex and Jess, to avoid future confetti storms, synthesize the above, discuss with Vex and River, then write down a plan. But *not* on paper.

Or you might just try securing the lid on your recycle bin.

Budleigh

DON'T HOLD THE PHONE

Dear Budleigh,

Zoe, our new poodle, has a problem. Or maybe I have a problem. Or Society. The thing is, Zoe keeps stealing my cell phone and snuggling with it on her bed. She's not making calls. I checked the phone bill. Also, as you can see in the photo, when she takes my phone, she surrounds her bed with her dried dog food bits. What's that all about? She doesn't act threatened or fearful. If anything, she seems a bit surprised that I want the phone back.

Guidance would be appreciated, Budleigh. And preferably soon. I've a super important Zoom meeting today at 4 p.m. I really need that phone!

Thanks, but don't bother texting.

Caryn, Michigan

Dear Caryn,

Zoe is just playing a game with you. A dark and dangerous game. But before we explore that, and possibly recommend martial arts training, let's better understand this behavior that Giants call "stealing" and Canines define as "adding to my permanent on-loan collection."

Some breeds are naturally inclined to liberate objects technically not their own. In addition to Retrievers, these Canines include:

- English Con Hound
- Australian Cattle Rustler
- Embezzlington Terrier
- Looterdoodle
- Bearded or Soft-coated Swipe
- Doberman Ponzi
- The U.S. Department of Justice

Security bars, a burner phone, a minefield of Kibbles – these set the Standard Poodle apart as a trained espionage agent.

But *all* dogs take things. Why? Because Giants have all the cool stuff. Had both species access to quality goods at affordable prices, an equitable barter system would have evolved from the moment Ancient Wolf first nicked an Ancient Barbecued Pork Chop off the Ancient Countertop of Ancient Giant.

Food, of course, tops the Canine list of Most-Confiscated-Items-Left-Too-Close-To-The-Table's-Edge. However, as a professionally licensed Canine, I can't advise Giants on how to safeguard their food because all the other dogs would hurt me.

In addition to food, Canines are keen to emancipate clothing: socks, underwear, shoes, casual evening wear, even coats up to a men's size 46 long. The attraction is their Giant's odor, which is pleasing, and their lack of style, which is embarrassing.

But mostly Canines crave toys, which they define as everything not food or clothing. And preferably with a knot in the middle.

Caryn, I understand your concern, perhaps even guilt over Zoe's behavior. But let me assure you that yes, it's all your fault. And I mean that in a positive, supportive way. As a Giant, you have one job, Caryn. *One job!* That is to anticipate Zoe's every need, indulge her every whim, and provide her every amusement.

Is that more than one job? I don't do math.

I sense that the lines of communication between you and Zoe have broken down. These are easy to repair unless you have Comcast. Let me suggest a role-playing exercise in which I'll play Zoe, and you, the part of every Giant in existence.

GIANT CARYN: "Zoe, dearest, have you once again appropriated my cell phone? Although this disturbs me on several levels, I'm sure that your intentions were honorable and that somehow, this is my own doing."

ZOE: "Why are you talking like that?"

GIANT CARYN: "Perhaps in my typical Giant naiveté I am neglecting your needs, sweet Zoe. Perhaps in your adorable, almost primal way, the procurement of my mobile device speaks to your perceived sense of alienation?"

Negotiating the return of stolen property from a possessive dog can be tricky. Especially if you're a mouse.

ZOE: "Your phone was by my cookies. We were out of cookies."

GIANT CARYN: "As I approach to retrieve my cellular device, my darling Zoe, I note that you have strewn your dry dog food hither and yon. I can only say I am confused and 'ewwwww!'"

ZOE: "When they crunch, I know you're coming."

GIANT CARYN: "Thank you, wise Zoe, for so cheerfully relinquishing my wireless communications mechanism. Can I provide you with anything that will further amuse and entertain you?"

ZOE: "What size coat is that? A 46 long?"

Budleigh

Zooming Isn't Like Running

Hey, Budleigh!

Is this social distancing as hard on dogs as on us Giants? When I take Edde, my big goof, on a stroll, I keep six feet from other dog walkers. They keep six feet from me. Edde cuts that in half by lunging. So does the opposing dog. So, what's that now, like seven, eight inches apart? It's exhausting. And a lot of math!

How are you staying in contact with your fellow Canines? Do you find Zoom useful, or is lack of thumbs a hindrance? Large keypads are available.

Hope to see you in the chat room. But wash your paws!

Emil and Edde, both big goofs

Dear Big Goofs,

This pandemic reminds us that Canines and Giants have much in common besides Netflix. We are gregarious, social animals that need to interact with our own kind. Both species are vulnerable to despair without familiar contact, without friendly communication, without ravioli stuffed with ricotta.

For Giants, Zoom is arguably the greatest communications advancement since yelling. Zoom is an easy, reliable cloud platform for video and audio conferencing, collaboration, chat, and webinars across mobile devices, desktops, telephones, and room systems, as I understand it.

OK, I *don't* understand it. It's written on this card my unpaid intern *Per Se* just handed me. Well, read to me. I don't understand writing either.

What I *do* understand is that shelter-in-place Giants unaccustomed to life in … *The Shelter*…use Zoom to reach out to other Giants if only to say, "Wait! What does *this* button—" before suddenly disconnecting.

For dogs, Zoom tools like multiscreens, video chat, and screen sharing are worthless without a smell feature

However, the communications tools offered to Canines by the Zoom corporation are no better than what's available at any publicly traded dog park.

LABRADOODLE: "Can you hear me over there? I can hear you! So, can you hear me?"

BORDER COLLIE: "I can hear you!"

LABRADOODLE: "Great! Well then … Hi!"

BORDER COLLIE: "You should come over here. There's this fabulous tree!"

LABRADOODLE: "My Giant won't let me get closer. You might have the Co-bid Papyrus. The Crow-Hidden-Iris. You know, that thing we'll catch unless we hide in the basement behind the furnace?"

TERRIER: "Bet I could catch it! And *kill* it! Even if it burrows in the garden."

LABRADOODLE: "Oh, hi! Can you hear me?"

BORDER COLLIE: "C'mere! You won't believe this tree—"

TERRIER: "Can't. Giant here has me on the short leash. And the Choke Collar of Servitude."

STANDARD POODLE: "Me too! It's like puppy school all over again."

LABRADOODLE: "Oh, hi! Can *you* hear me?"

STANDARD POODLE: "Don't know. Did you say anything?"

BORDER COLLIE: "I can *not* herd under these conditions."

STANDARD POODLE: "So, how's everybody's butts?"

BORDER COLLIE: "Nothing new to report."

TERRIER: "Same old, same old."

GERMAN SHEPHERD: "Hey, sorry I'm late. My Yelly Giant was having technical issues with Zoom. What'd I miss?"

STANDARD POODLE: "Just the butts update. Oh, and *he's* having audio problems."

LABRADOODLE: "Hi! Can you hear—"

BORDER COLLIE: "Come see my PowerPoint presentation. It's on this tree over here."

STANDARD POODLE: "What's this 'Zoom' thing? My Giants are giving it a lot of attention."

TERRIER: "Mine too! I think Zoom's a puppy."

STANDARD POODLE: "A puppy with technical issues?"

GERMAN SHEPHERD: "Well, it lives in their laptop."

TERRIER: "How come we never see this puppy?"

All ponder quietly.

BORDER COLLIE: "He's shy?"

LABRADOODLE: "Poor little guy. I'll bet *he* could hear me!"

BORDER COLLIE: "Those Giants should bring him to the dog park. Show him this tree."

MALTESE: "I can make that happen. I'm a lap dog. He's in a lap*top*. Twinsies!"

GERMAN SHEPHERD: "That makes sense."

BORDER COLLIE: "So, let's meet this pup—what's his name? Zoom? Bring him here tomorrow. By this tree."

GERMAN SHEPHERD: "Sure! I'll make my Giants walk him outside the laptop."

TERRIER: *(Muttering)* Probably on a short leash. And spiked collar."

LABRADOODLE: "I think you *all* can hear me now! So ... Bye!"

Budleigh

Sheltering Outside
the Shelter

Dear Budleigh,

In these pandemic times, I'm confident that your focus is on safety and hygiene because you're medically trained, although you don't use toilet paper.

We Giants are trying to maintain that same focus, but it ain't easy! Worry runs high. Fortunately, many of us have you guys to cuddle. I hope that isn't straining the Giant/Canine relationship. If so, look, there's gonna be an extra cookie in it for all of you, I guarantee!

Be well and stock up on poop bags!

Charles, Ft. Worth TX

Dear Charles,

I'm still trying to wrap my teeth around this pandemic. I wasn't schooled in the Sciences. Or anything, really, if we're to believe my report card from Intermediate Obedience Class. (Comments: "Budleigh doesn't heel up to potential.")

To better understand the COVID 19 Coronavirus, I turned to my science advisor, Jellybean, an Appenzeller Sennenhund—a breed that also sounds like a virus.

JELLYBEAN: "Research indicates that this virus does not infect Canines. That's the upside."

BUDLEIGH: "So, there's no downside!"

JELLYBEAN: "Well, it's highly contagious among Giants."

BUDLEIGH: "Uh-huh …"

JELLYBEAN: "Especially the elderly or health-compromised."

BUDLEIGH: "Uh-huh, uh-huh. And … so?"

Anxious dogs self soothe by ordering meals online. A lot!

JELLYBEAN: "That could affect our food supply."

BUDLEIGH: "Aaaand by 'our food supply' you mean …?"

JELLYBEAN: "*Your* food supply."

BUDLEIGH: "*Why are we still talking?* Alert Whole Foods!"

After assurances that supply lines are secure, chipmunks remain plentiful, and toilet paper is … What is toilet paper, anyway? … I gained a better perspective on how best to fight this *pathogen.* (Latin for "Use a Kleenex! Jeez!") During this crisis, Canines are uniquely positioned to support their Giants. Likewise, Giants are well-positioned to support *other* Giants. Here are some tips.

Handwashing is a most powerful weapon against germs, which Jellybean and many health experts agree are too small to bite in their throats. Giants should thoroughly scrub their hands with soap before touching their face. Ideally, Giants would scrub their hands before touching *my* face, but let's not quibble. This is war!

Hands should be scrubbed long enough to sing the Happy Birthday Song twice. *Important* note: Just *singing* is not enough! Soap and water are essential.

Yeah, that one surprised me, too.

Here's a tactic for Canines to remind your Giant to wash. On walkies, when Giant bends down to pick up poop, subtly pee on his hands. Interestingly, Giants don't find that subtle. They scrub for the rest of the day. I've been doing that to my Yelly Giant for years, but just for yucks.

Social distancing is another effective weapon to limit the spread of pathogens. Giants should space themselves six feet from each other. That's the length of three to twelve dogs, depending on the breed. Also, on whether they're in a "Sit! Stay!" or stretched out asleep. This distance can vary in the U.K. and other countries that use the metric system.

Coughing and sneezing spread germs. So lacking Kleenex or a hanky, do it into your elbow. Giants might find this vulgar, but for Canines it's *impossible,* what with all our elbows, many of which face the wrong direction. So, Giants, be grateful for your gift.

Finally, obey shelter-in-place precautions. Naturally, I cringed from this directive because of the words "shelter" and "obey." However, it's proved harmless to me and emotionally therapeutic for my Giants.

GIANT 1: "That's it, hon! We've watched everything on Netflix."

GIANT 2: "Darn!"

GIANT 1: "'Darn?' I don't think you appreciate the gravity. We've WATCHED! EVERYTHING! On NETFLIX!"

GIANT 2: "I'll get the ice cream!"

BUDLEIGH: "Don't get up! I just got your lap the way I like it."

GIANT 2: "*You* get it, Dave, because … you know … I've got a Budleigh."

GIANT 1: "He's been *such* a comfort."

BUDLEIGH: "Go ahead, pet my coat. It's extra shiny, smooth and lustrous."

GIANT 2: "His fur's gotten *so* soft and warm."

BUDLEIGH: "I'm eating more eggs. And thanks!"

GIANT 1: "He's so affectionate lately. Like he senses that we're anxious and wants to console us. Don't you, li'l Budleigh? Oh yes, you do! Yes, you do!"

BUDLEIGH: "Can we flip on Animal Planet or something? You're wearing out my coat."

GIANT 1: "I'm gonna give him an extra egg, then cuddle him some more. He loves it when I scratch his ears and stroke his muzzle."

BUDLEIGH: "Just wash your hands. Or do I need to pee on 'em?"

Budleigh

IS IT A TERRIER WORLD? IS IT?

Dear Budleigh, (I don't believe that is your real name!)

Explain to me why on Earth a terrier is better than a noble black Labrador who happens to have the name Louie, weighs 67 pounds, loves to watch baseball and Seinfeld, is a good bromance buddy, lives in Michigan, makes a wicked rice pilaf, does my taxes (all forms and schedules), avoids polarizing political discussions, and generally brings peace and joy to our household?

Go ahead, make my day and explain that to me, brillo boy!

Yours, Minnesota Twins Fan Theatre Guy

Dear Minnie,

Labs are nice, too.

Budleigh

"Labradors are wonderful dogs! Did I say wonderful?
I meant fabulous! The Best! Please, don't wake them!"

BUDLEIGH ANALYZES THERAPY

Dear Budleigh,

I think that I'd make a good therapy dog. Is it hard to become one? I have my own harness. It has a pocket. Are there any further requirements?

FYI, my fur is soft.

Respectfully yours,

Baldur (as dictated to my Giant Mitch)

Dear Baldur,

My Yelly Giant often remarks that, "The best therapy dog comes in little, blue pills!" Then, he laughs. A lot! Sometimes cries.

He means, I assume, that to pursue this higher calling, canines must understand the difference between being a therapy dog, trained to provide comfort and affection, and a service dog, permitted to carry a concealed firearm.

According to the American Kennel Club (Motto: "Stay!"), therapy dog candidates should be naturally calm, friendly and affectionate. However, professional training is needed to mold a dog into a patient, adaptable companion or, in certain cases, a merciless killing machine. (See *The Manchurian Candidate.*)

Decades-long scientific research reduced to a 20-second news clip proves the benefits to Giants of a therapy dog – lower blood pressure and heart rate, reduced anxiety, and increased levels of endorphins and oxytocins – two ingredients normally found in shoes.

Therapy dogs are comfortable in a variety of facility settings, like hospital wards and nursing homes. There, Giants depend on them to share their serene character. That's an awesome responsibility. So, before deciding to train, Baldur, ask yourself, "Am I truly tranquil, or do I just sleep a lot?"

At the dog park, Budleigh and Brisby hone their skills at staying calm – possibly comatose.

Frankly, I'd have made a fine therapy dog but for, you'll pardon the expression, "obedience class." What a scam! Nothing but cliques made up of Hipsters, Mean Girls and Golden Retrievers. And if you don't fit in, if you're a free spirit, if you bite just *one* little instructor – and not even that deep – they label you "terrier."

That's a brand that stays with you; probably embossed on one of those jingly things on your collar. And because of it, you'll never be a therapy dog. Or hold public office. Or work with explosives.

So, think long and hard, Baldur. You face a tough road ahead with no promise of a better harness – or even a pocket.

Budleigh

CAN'T WE ALL
JUST GET ALONG?

Dear Budleigh,

I am a Miniature Poodle. I want to be friends with other dogs, but I lunge at them barking ferociously. How can I curb this behavior?

And should I?

Thank you!

Pebbles

Dear Pebbles,

I feel your pain. Or might if you're biting, too.

You're being far too hard on yourself when, of course, Society is to blame. I'm not sure who "Society" is, but my Yelly Giant blames Society a lot. I think Society is that Giant Steve down the street who doesn't return power tools.

Pebbles, you ask how to curb this behavior. I ask you, "Why?" Lunging and barking ferociously is just one dog's way of saying to another, "Can I give you my business card?"

Giants often perceive lunging and barking ferociously as aggressive behavior. I think that's because of our fangs, which they often perceive as razor sharp.

I've never really needed to lunge and bark ferociously at other dogs because, since I'm a terrier, everyone does what I want. But I know that a lot of dogs share your issue, so I brought it up for discussion at the dog park.

GOLDEN RETRIEVER: "So, what if another dog lunges or barks? Can I still bring 'em things? Like my brush? Or maybe the leash? Or that squeezy, screechy thing that my Giant says is blue, whatever that means?"

BOXER: "Barking? Yeah, that gets old fast, but I usually overlook it. But lunging? I don't trust a dog that doesn't lunge. To me, that's a big, red flag. Well, I'm *told* it's red. I've no way of knowing."

On first meeting, dogs often dare each other to cross a line.
Usually made with pee.

SCHNOODLE: "What's a French Poodle? Is that like French toast? I'm hungry!"

YORKSHIRE TERRIER: "Wait! You said a *Miniature* Poodle? How miniature? Smaller than me, right? 'Cause then I say, 'lunge and bark away, brother!'"

BERNESE MOUNTAIN DOG: "When we bark in the mountains, it echoes for miles. No lunging, though. Too dangerous!"

PUG: "You don't know what a mountain is, do you?"

BERNESE MOUNTAIN DOG: "Do *too!* My Giants got me one. It's rawhide!"

PUG: "That's not a mountain!"

BERNESE MOUNTAIN DOG: "Yeah? *Yeah?* Well, maybe *you're* not a mountain!"

PUG: "Maybe *you're* not!"

BOXER: "Lunge at him! Lunge at him!"

GOLDEN RETRIEVER: "Wait! I'll fetch my squeezy, screechy thing!"

SCHNOODLE: "Am I the *only* one who's hungry?"

Some valuable tips there, Pebbles. Just sorry there weren't more, but I couldn't hear over all the barking.

Budleigh

MARK OF THE HALLMARK

Hello, Budleigh!

Big fan of Hallmark Christmas Movies here. I'm excited that 40 new titles are slated over the holiday season, which according to Hallmark began last July.

While Hallmark's programming is enjoyable, several issues distract me:

1. *July?*
2. *In their movies that feature a dog, it's always a terrier.*
3. *Is that a union thing, terriers?*

You seem to have your paw on the pulse of the entertainment industry, Budleigh. Any insights into why terriers rather than other breeds? Um … I'm asking for a friend. Who's curled in my lap, sighing sadly.

Happy holidays!

Jennie C., her friend, and all the Whos down in Whoville

Dear Jennie and friend,

What a wonderful tradition is Hallmark holiday movie season! My Giants and their Giant Relatives gather 'round the television, laugh and cry, share memories, and, with any luck, spill food on the floor. Truly, a Season of Grabbing.

As to the abundance of terriers in Hallmark movies, let me clear up a misconception. Terriers never unionize. Fiercely independent, we barely cooperate with each other unless in pursuit of prey or a criminal enterprise. Unions serve best for breeds like Golden Retrievers, Labradors, and other apple-polishers.

Oh, and fish.

Like many of us, terriers closely identify with specific Hallmark movie characters.

Although unaffiliated with work unions, terriers have made impressive inroads in the movie business in the decades since Asta first peed on William Powell's leg. Today, these plucky, determined Canines can be found in every stratum of the industry, from security to — well, mostly security — although some are actors and a few write.

Like me.

Oh, I'm glad you asked!

Currently in development is a Hallmark holiday movie script I wrote with the minor assistance of my intern, *Per Se*, who serves as thumbs. I know that many readers – Giants and Canines – dream of breaking into the movie industry despite those terriers working security. Scriptwriting, especially a Hallmark movie, can provide an easy back door into the profession for Giants and a convenient doggie door for Canines.

Begin by creating an appropriate Hallmark Movie Title. Such a title is warm, welcoming, cute, nonjudgmental, nonpolitical, noncontroversial, non-swears, and short enough so there's room for a product placement. Generally, titles follow this pattern: "A (*something*) for a (*something*)" or "A (*something*) (*something*) Holiday!" where at least one of the *somethings* is mistletoe.

That's it! You're done! Put your feet or paws up, sip a hot cup of mistletoe, and wait for your check. Sure, you could write some scenes, maybe a bit of dialogue, but that's usually done by a production assistant in post.

However, if you're fiercely independent, plucky, and nonunion like me, you'll prefer to produce a complete movie script. Mine is autobiographical and a true story which I made up. The title is "Tinsel for a Terrier." They changed it from my original title "Ho, Ho, Homeless" which trended poorly among the 25- to 30-year-old Giant demographic. And also working dogs.

"Tinsel for a Terrier" is a deeply thoughtful story of a shelter dog searching for a home. I'd be crying right now if Canine tear ducts were capable of responding to emotional stimuli. Add in the requisite Hallmark Movie Giant couple haphazardly orbiting each other; mix with a scattering of predictable holiday plot points; then bake in a 450-degree oven for 40 minutes and Arf! There's your script.

Here's a preview:

GIANT BOY: "Look, Karen! Isn't this the Christmas ornament that your mother misplaced when she moved out of your family home to care for your ailing aunt, leaving you saddled with the threat of eviction, even though you never complain and instead work to expand your singing career while caring for your unbelievably innocent 12-year-old nephew who, surprisingly, still believes in Santa Claus?"

GIANT GIRL: "It is! Wherever did you find it?"

GIANT BOY: "At the church's Christmas rummage sale where I volunteer all year 'round, as well as making substantial but secret donations."

TINSEL TERRIER: "That's my trainer over there! See him? Off camera, there? Watch him! He'll give you a cookie!"

GIANT GIRL: "Thank you, Fred. And I never want to see you again!"

TINSEL TERRIER: "Hi, trainer! *Hi!*"

GIANT BOY: "Why, Karen? I don't understand, although I'm sure it's obvious."

GIANT GIRL: "Because I overheard part, though not all, of your conversation with your British butler with whom you mysteriously share a small but lavishly furnished apartment, when you told him that you'd interfere with my singing career. Goodbye!"

TINSEL TERRIER: "Trainer wants me to wrap your feet with my leash. Sorry! Do you have a cookie? Sorry!"

GIANT BOY: "It seems that little Evergreen here has drawn us into an inescapable embrace, although he weighs only 17 pounds. But now you must listen to me explain the part of the conversation that you missed, which is that I would NEVER interfere with your etcetera, etcetera."

GIANT GIRL: "Oh, Fred! I love you!"

TINSEL TERRIER: "Does trainer look mad? I hope he's not mad."

GIANT BOY: "I love you, too, Karen. Oh, and my real name is Frederik von Henrik d'Pufferi. I'm crown prince of the community-sized kingdom of Tinystan and heir to a lavish product-placed Lexis!"

GIANT GIRL: "And I just learned that I'm heir to an enormous estate Mother neglected to mention. I love you … Fred!"

TINSEL TERRIER: "I'm being cued to lick you. Sorry! Gotta lick you!"

GIANT BOY & GIRL: "Oh, Evergreen! And *Lexis!*"

A potent script, right? But honestly, I just want to direct!

Budleigh

It's In the Bag!

Dear Budleigh,

What's the best bag for a dog? My sweetie Brussels Griffon, Tinker, commutes everywhere with me in her suede faux fur-lined carrier. But she's an uncompromising fashionista! And a style trendsetter, judging by the head-turning envy her presence evokes.

The problem is that the fringe on her carrier – I call it her runway – is looking a bit ratty. And worse, passé! She deserves better. Well, the best!

I'm desperate for your voguish advice on her replacement carrier. A tote that will part crowds when they see her coming. Something savvy and sassy and cleanly fashion forward. Otherwise, we might as well just outfit her in a velour tracksuit and platform pumps and call it 2002.

Ewww!

J. J. and Tinker, #MadShoppingInNY

Dear J. J. and Tinker,

Happy to assist. Fashion is my life! Just after killing chipmunks. Oh, and tug-tug.

Full disclosure, though: With the exception of my collar, I've never worn any fashions. Yes, there was a brief afternoon when my Giants and I "discussed" a no-pull dog harness. That didn't end well. For anyone.

However, I'm not without a keen and very personal fashion sense. Like Tinker's carrier, I'm fur lined. And there's nothing faux about mine. Can Michael Kors make that claim? I think not!

While style is important, for dogs, comfort must hold sway. Not all fit in a personal carrier. (*See Clifford, the Big, Red Hernia.*) Giants first must ask themselves: 1. "How small is my dog?"; 2. "Seriously? That small?"; and 3. "Wait! Is that even a dog? It has six legs!"

Having correctly calculated your dog's dimensions, and fumigated your apartment — *Ewww!* — choose a tote that is roomy, protective, and rent controlled. Let me explore the pros and cons of several styles of carriers without actually getting inside one.

Dog backpack and front pack carriers, while popular and functional, serve different purposes. Roomy and secure, backpacks allow your canine to observe where he's just been. Front packs do the same, provided you walk backwards. Not recommended for use by Giants with fewer than three legs.

Another option is the carrier sling, which is at once stylish for you and humiliating for your dog. Essentially, the sling is a strap with a pocket, much like an athletic supporter undergarment with room for credit cards. Oh, and a dog. Few professional sportsmen use athletic supporters this way, or if so, won't admit it.

**A chic tote carries all accessories needed by the modern
Canine on the go!**

An ever-popular choice for Giants and Canines is the chic and
sophisticated designer shoulder carrier. Spacious for dogs and
offering plenty of storage, many modern shoulder carriers also
are *ergonomic*, meaning they bear live young, yet are aquatic.

Least attractive is the "puppy purse," a minimalist harness that
fits a small canine, legs dangling, and includes a carry handle on
the back for transporting the dog. I don't consider this an
acceptable carrier for the same reasons that it was outlawed by
the Geneva Convention.

Feeling besieged by too many fashion options for Tinker, J. J.? Just take your time. I'm sure that she's blessed with a figure that looks *fabulous* in everything!

Well, not cap sleeves. Who does?

Budleigh

OH, GREAT …
ANOTHER NEW COLLAR

Dear Mr. Budleigh,

For a Christmas stocking stuffer, I'm thinking of buying a new collar. Any advice?

Carrie, South Bend, Indiana

Dear Ms. Bend-Indiana,

Is the collar for you or a dog? That's not clear. If it's for a dog, then yes, I can advise. If it's for you, seek professional help immediately! But I'm guessing it's for a dog, right?

Giants love to buy collars for their dogs, especially during the holidays. I heard that in the weekend following Thanksgimme Day, more than 154 million Giants went shopping. I don't know if they *all* were buying me new collars or just chipped in for one really, *really* nice one. But I wish they'd asked me first. I don't want a new collar. No dogs do.

Sorry I said "dog do," but this issue is that important.

First, I know I speak for all dogs – especially the ones that are afraid of terriers – in discouraging Giants from arbitrarily "upgrading" collars. My Giants are always discussing upgrading stuff, like Wi-Fi, batteries, apps, family members. I don't know if my collar has those things, but it would explain the jingling.

Frankly, dogs are not impressed with upgrades they can't chew. If a collar isn't in need of repair, why replace it? Me? I believe in following that old canine adage: "If it ain't broke, I haven't gotten to it yet."

Second, Giants believe new collars make dogs "cute." Look, I gotta trust 'em on that one. I can't see my collar. I'm not even convinced it exists! My Giants have tried to show me in the big mirror, but I'm just too distracted by that weird dog they keep inside there. The one that moves exactly like me. Brrrrr! Creepy!

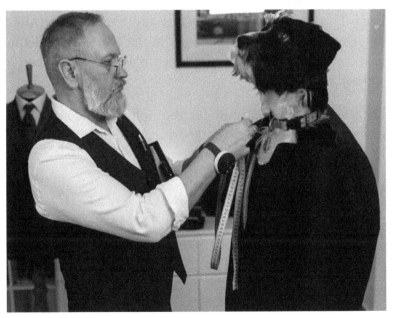

"Clothes make the dog.
And yes, *of course* I was invited to my prom! Rude!"

So, who am I to judge? Sure, everyone agrees that I'm cute. But is "cute" all a dog should strive for? What about "loyal"? OK, that one's a given. I mean, we're dogs. Still, there's "charming," "intelligent," "fearless." Collars need to build a dog's reputation. We all can't be Golden Retrievers. Jeez, they're insufferable! Why do they even have collars?

Choose a collar that helps a dog make a bold, defining statement: "I hardly ever eat poop!"; "This kitchen floor is mine!"; "Golden Retrievers are insufferable!"

But please, stick with collars. None of my Giants wants to face another "plaid coat" fiasco. I couldn't shred that blunder fast enough!

Third – and we're at third, aren't we? I don't do that counting thing. Third, don't bother gift wrapping a collar. Or anything. Ever! That only disappoints Giants and puzzles dogs. More thoughtful would be to shove a gift in the garbage, then let us nose around 'til we find it. Or a turkey carcass. Either is appreciated.

Look, you're our Giants. Any gift from you – a new collar, bacon treats, even a bully stick (You know that's a bull's penis, right? Just want to be clear.) – will make us happy.

Especially a chipmunk!

Budleigh

BUDLEIGH ADDRESSES A ROYAL PAIN

Dear Budleigh,

I was gobsmacked – isn't that what the British say, gobsmacked? – when Prince Harry and wife Meghan announced they were stepping down from their royal duties. I thought that only happened when angry peasants carrying torches stormed your castle. Harry's way was so more civilized. And hardly anyone was hanged!

But I'm concerned. Not for me but for my own personal royal family, which is Queenie, our King Charles Spaniel. As her breed implies, Queenie views herself as integral to the British Monarchy, and as such is 1,487th in line to the throne of England. Will Harry's decision move Queenie closer to ascending to head of state? If so, will that interfere with her butterfly-chasing responsibilities. Also, does the high office come with a lap? She demands these be sorted out quickly!

By the way, Budleigh, you have a certain aristocratic profile. Is it possible you're descended from royalty?

To the Queen!

Andrea, Personal Advisor and Dresser to the Queen, Queenie

Dear Andrea and QQ,

During my early days in the shelter, canine "lifers" who mocked my Hapsburg jaw were quickly introduced to its weaponized teeth. Admittedly, I'm sensitive about my profile. Learning to be comfortable in my own fur took the patience of two devoted Giants, my secured ownership of their home, and access to cornbread.

A *lot* of cornbread!

So, I'm sympathetic to the awesome game of tug-tug between duty and lifestyle faced by Queenie, and to a lesser extent, Harry.

Yet, Queenie's dilemma is not unique. A surprising number of canines were bred to the manner born. Or at least to lounge on the bed.

These breeds include:

- Canadian Crown Royal Russian Oligarch
- Great Mimzie Pimzie
- Border Terrier Without Borders
- Downton Abbeydale
- Miniature Mimzie Pimzie
- Curly Coated Royal Doulton with Matching Silver Tea Service
- Mimzie Pimzie Whimsy Bimzie
- Duke

Despite their royal lineage, confusion abounds among dogs about the role of canines in the British Monarchy, the strength of their claims to the throne, and the correct interpretation of the term "walkies!" For clarity, I consulted the hive mind that is the dog pack at the local park.

GREAT PYRENEES: "...so you're saying that if Queen Elizabeth is, you know, put down, her Corgis assume the throne?"

ENGLISH SHEEPDOG: "No, no, no! Well, yes. They're out of the direct line of succession, but they still get to nap on the throne. That's in the Magna Carta."

GREAT PYRENEES: "Are Pyrenees still in the running? We *really* are Great!"

BERNESE MOUNTAIN DOG: "Whoa! Hold the phone there, Lady! My Giant says the Pyrenees are a mountain range. And *I'm* a mountain range. Do I have to spell it out for you 'cause, ya know, I can't spell."

ENGLISH SHEEPDOG: "All this quarreling is pointless. The royal line of succession? It's all in the Magna Carta!"

PUG: "You keep saying that. What is this 'Magna Carta'?"

ENGLISH SHEEPDOG: (*Long pause*) "It's a lot of ... spelling."

BUDLEIGH: "OK, let's all try to stay on task without being herded. (*To Sheepdog*) No offense."

ENGLISH SHEEPDOG: "We're good!"

BUDLEIGH: "Queenie wonders about her position now in the royal hierarchy. Does she take up residence in the palace or just move into Prince Harry's old crate?"

BRISBY THE SCHNOODLE: "Who's Prince Harry?"

For royal dogs, the public scrutiny of palace life is
outweighed by stylish bling.

BORDER COLLIE: "I know! I know! He was a *Working* Royal.
That would have put him in my dog show breed group. Like the
Duke of Gloucester!"

BRISBY THE SCHNOODLE: "That's a cheese, right?
Gloucester? I'm *so* hungry!"

ENGLISH SHEEPDOG: "A lot of royals are cheese related: the
Duke of Lancashire; the Duchess of Leicestershire; the Low-fat
Earl of Pepper Jack —"

PUG: "—The Duchess of Corn Dog!"

ENGLISH SHEEPDOG: "No, she's less cheese related than batter-dipped and deep fried."

GREAT PYRENEES: "The Earl of Sandwich?"

ENGLISH SHEEPDOG: "Yes, I suppose."

GREAT PYRENEES: "*Count* Chocula!'

BRISBY THE SCHNOODLE: "Chocolate's bad for us."

BORDER COLLIE: "Wait! I got one! Chicken a la … *King!* I went to obedience school with one 'a those!

BUDLEIGH: "So, the Royal Family are all about … snackies?"

ENGLISH SHEEPDOG: "Of course! And to a lesser degree staggering wealth, international influence, and historical prestige."

BRISBY THE SCHNOODLE: "Am I the *only* one who's hungry?"

So, here is the takeaway, Andrea: If the Fates decree that Queenie ascend to the royal throne, remind her always that with Great Power comes Great Snackies!

Budleigh

How the Dogs Are Voting

Dear Budleigh,

Assuming that you're not a registered voter, have you any advice for us Giants on the U.S. elections? We seem to be making quite a hash of it.

You dogs seem to agree on a pack leader without being overwhelmed by confused caucuses, authoritarian threats, and malicious foreign intervention. (Unless, you know, Russian Wolfhounds?)

What are Canines doing right that Giants are doing wrong? If you've a solution, you can have that hash I mentioned!

Help me, Obi-Wan KenoBudleigh! You're my only hope!

JP, New Hampshire

Dear JP,

By a happy coincidence, elections for Alpha are coming up soon in our dog park. Much like Giant elections, campaigning has been spirited, robust, and in a few tragic cases, feral (usually just among candidates who were off-leash.)

The job of the Alpha is a serious one, often described by Canines as "daunting" and by Giants as "adorable." As the pack's representative, the Alpha must speak to Giants in the unified voice of all Canines. That's best done at 2 a.m. in a shrill, grating howl.

But it takes more than a candidate's annoying whine to win an election. It demands a confident voting process that is scrupulously honest, above suspicion, and clean as a fresh poop bag. Such is the only way to guarantee a turnout on election day in the dog park of an electorate as informed as it is confused.

Dog park debates present candidates many challenges, such as microphones.

At dog park entrance check-in:

BEARDED COLLIE ELECTION JUDGE: "Name?"

AIREDALE: (*Long pause*) "What do you mean?"

BEARDED COLLIE: "Your name! What's your name?"

AIREDALE: "Well … that depends who's calling me."

BEARDED COLLIE: "… What?"

AIREDALE: "My Food Giant calls me 'Sweetie,' but my Yelly Giant yells at me, 'C'mere!' And the Little Giants? Sometimes one calls me, 'He's mine!' and the other, 'No! He's mine!' Then they both call me 'Mooooom!' It's all very confusing."

STANDARD POODLE PRECINCT JUDGE: "I'll handle this! (*To voter*) We need your name to check that you're registered to vote in this park."

AIREDALE: "Ohhhh! That makes sense!"

Long pause. Growing group of dogs wait. Some sit. Others yawn.

STANDARD POODLE: "Sooooo … name?"

AIREDALE: "Well … depends who's—"

STANDARD POODLE: "We're just gonna call you 'Absentee.'"

AIREDALE: "I like that!"

STANDARD POODLE: "Next!"

Inside the park, as candidates meet and greet.

ROTTWEILER: "Hi! Vote for me or I'll kill you!"

AIREDALE: "Uh … OK."

BEAGLE: "Wait! Why?"

ROTTWEILER: "Did I say 'Kill?' Sorry! I meant, 'Usher in a Golden Era of Peace, Prosperity and those Little Meaty Chews.'"

SCHNOODLE: "What's 'vote?'"

GOLDEN RETRIEVER: "Hi! Vote for me! I'll be your best friend! Or don't. I'll *still* be your best friend. Can I go get you something? Anything? Even if it's heavy!"

BEAGLE: "Thanks, we're good."

SCHNOODLE: "Again with this 'vote.' What's *that* all about?"

BEAGLE: "My Giant says that we vote for what we want, what's important, what's good for us all."

SCHNOODLE: "Can I vote for peanut butter?"

BEAGLE: "Let me check this pamphlet ..."

These Canines' calm, thoughtful, deliberate approach to electing their leader or choosing a sandwich spread offers valuable advice for you Giants. Use it well! And before you ask, thank you but no, I will *never* run for Alpha. I've all the Peace, Prosperity and Little Meaty Chews I need.

Budleigh

JUST HOW INFRA IS OUR STRUCTURE?

Hey, Budleigh!

So, when the village rebuilt the sidewalk in front of our house, they had to take down my silver maple tree. Or more precisely, Kippy's silver maple tree, as he has been – how shall I phrase this – nurturing it 2 to 3 times a day for eight years.

He's handled the removal pretty well, although it's shaken his faith in government. Now they've upended Kippy's favorite street sign at the end of the block, which he's also nurtured all these years. His world is coming apart. He's outwardly stoic, but instead of gazing at me with the face of an adoring pup, now he glares with the cold, dead eyes of a mob hit man who's been double-crossed.

Is that normal?

Sleeping with One Eye Open,

Dale, Oak Park, Illinois

Dear Dale and Kippy,

Kippy's right. Government has failed. So screams my Yelly Giant who throws a *lot* of stuff at Anderson Cooper.

But there's a bigger picture. One to be gleaned from watching not just my Giants' news programming, but their baking shows, and home shopping. Oh, and that one where everyone gets chopped up with swords and there's a dragon.

Through this research, I've learned about how infrastructure crumbles leaving roads and bridges in disrepair, cakes and pies overbaked, reasonably priced zircon necklaces abandoned, and villages decimated by dragon fire.

My takeaway: Government hasn't just failed. It's failed *dogs*. Yet another reason I choose not to vote. And snarl at pollsters!

Vigilant watch dogs prepare to encounter ... Infrastructure!

I agree with Kippy. What's the value in uprooting a perfectly pee-worthy tree, upending a Canine-endorsed street sign when so much of this deteriorating nation could collapse with a single robust sneeze? Is *that* the point of Infrastructure Week, which is like Shark Week only fictional?

Forgive my howling, but this has become a deeply personal issue since they tore out my puppy swings.

The puppy-faced toddler swings on the playground in the park didn't belong to *me* so much as they belonged to the world. But they *looked* like me. Decorated with black ears and black-and-white muzzles, the bucket swings resembled my skull with a Giant child sitting inside.

Not as spooky as it sounds.

Because I passed the playground to and from the dog park, Giant children treated me as a celebrity, giggling shyly, tentatively petting me, or trying to sit in my skull. I accepted this attention as I enjoy Giant children, even when they're off leash.

Then the Government tore out the toddler swings and leveled the playground. Yet, Anderson Cooper said nothing!

New equipment has been installed including featureless swings, a spinning thing, a bigger spinning thing, a thing that doesn't spin but has knobs, and a slide that, alone in the night, spins and grows knobs.

Nothing looks like me anymore. That's racism! Species-ism?

So yes, Dale, Kippy's response is perfectly normal. Quite restrained, even. Imagine how upset he'd be if Giant children no longer tried to sit in his skull.

Budleigh

Semper Canis!

Hey Budleigh!

How cool is it that a new line of postage stamps will honor the military's working canines? Have you seen them? They feature four breeds often used as military working dogs: German shepherd, Dutch shepherd, Labrador retriever, and Belgian Malinois.

Sadly, no Chihuahua mix like my Loki. Has the military considered training and deploying Chihuahua mixes? Loki would be ideal for covert missions where concealment and stealth are imperative. Unless it's against field mice near a bird feeder. Loki gets very emotional.

And what about terriers? Are you jealous?

Stay frosty!

Kevin B. and West Point Cadet hopeful Loki

(Courtesy U.S. Postal Service/Released)

Dear Kevin and Loki,

Jealous? More like envious. Proud, brave, and uncomplaining despite having to wear harnesses, our fearless military warriors are trained in narcotics and explosives detection, search and rescue, security, and tracking.

**Military canine recruits deemed unfit for service
rarely are honored on stamps.**

I can steal socks from the laundry basket, but there seems little call for that skill set. Nonetheless, when I was young, I seriously considered a career in the military. As a shelter dog, I yearned to belong to something bigger than myself. Or at least bigger than my cage.

But while I demonstrated to the recruiter what I thought was appropriate aggressiveness, I lacked the stature, the sheer physical size required. I mean, I was in good shape. But look at those stamps! I'd never be as huge as a German or Dutch shepherd, Labrador retriever, or Belgian Malinois — a breed that is less a canine than a large piece of earthmoving equipment.

Also, I failed the psych evaluation. Twice.

Though humbled, I'm a steadfast supporter of military working dogs. And surprisingly, so is the U.S. Postal Service whose angry mail carriers would be within their rights to stuff dog-stamped mail down a sewer rather than deliver.

Respect, mail carriers! For now …

Loki, I won't dissuade you from pursuing a military career. War is unpredictable. Someday enemy skies might be filled with paratrooper Chihuahua peacekeeping forces. I hope world conflict never comes to that. But if it does, post that image on YouTube!

Meanwhile, take solace and pride that you're defending the home front. Field mice are implacable adversaries. As are cicadas, voles, and, under certain conditions, sprinkler heads.

And while we must admire the U.S. Postal Service, their actions might just be a feint. Keep your eyes on the mail slot!

Budleigh

WHAT'S BUGGING BUDLEIGH?

Dear Budleigh,

In a recent column you mentioned eating spiders, which got me thinking, "Ewwww!"

It also got me thinking about recent news video of a spider the size of a dinner plate — a dinner plate! — observed in the Amazon rainforest of Peru. It blatantly killed and ate an opossum as though perfectly aware – and dismissive – of YouTube.

Now I'm worried that legions of dinner plate-sized spiders are rapidly reproducing, then headed our way. And frankly, there ain't a border wall big enough!

As you're comfortable with a certain level of spiders, any advice on where I should hide?

Warmest regards,

Cowering Beneath the Duvat, Burlington, VT

Dear Coward,

In typical Giant fashion you've reacted to overblown reports of "spiders the size of dinner plates" before asking, "Whose dinner?"

I spend a lot of time close to the ground and know that *all* spiders are the size of dinner plates if you get close enough. Conversely, coyotes are tiny when they're *waaay* over there. Giant scientists refer to this phenomenon as, "I don't get that either." Then they avoid uncomfortable questions by moving their research to the Peruvian Amazon rainforest where cell phone reception is poor. And spiders *are* the size of dinner plates.

Among those scientists hiding in the rainforest was the University of Michigan team of biologists that encountered this rare, gigantic spider of the taxonomic infraorder Mygalomorphae (Latin for, "Are you *shitting* me?") This appears to be the first documented case of a spider eating an opossum, which while historic, didn't brighten the opossum's day. The scientists admit they were lucky to come across this encounter. Also lucky *they* were not opossums.

For rainforest scientists, an essential tool for measurement is a precisely calibrated dinner plate.

This might not be politically correct to say since I don't know what a "politically" is, but, you go, rare, gigantic Peruvian Mygalomorph!

Out of fear, ignorance and revulsion, many Giants disparage spiders as though they were coworkers. This might be due to spiders' extravagant number of appendages, although frankly they've no more legs than two dogs running side by side. I think it more a matter of the way spiders strut. Especially the big ones – like they're top of the card on a WWE pay per view.

"That's right! That's right!" they bluster. "I'm *the* predator! And your girlfriend's ugly! C'mon, you wanna piece a' me? Huh? Ya wanna piece?"

No, nobody wants a piece of that. Certainly not opossums.

As a predator myself, legally recognized in 23 states and the District of Columbia, I can respect, even admire spiders – from the gigantic Mygalomorph, due to its cunning, down to the common household arachnoid because they're so tasty.

So, my Peruvian Mygalomorph brethren, should you plan to emigrate I welcome you in the language of your homeland, "Vaya con carne!"

But be warned, amigo: I, too, am the size of a dinner plate.

Budleigh

DESTROY ALL MONSTERS!

Dear Budleigh,

Poolie eats cicadas. A lot of cicadas! Like more cicadas than any dog in the world. I've tried to stop her but she's fast. And a lot closer to the ground than me.

Are cicadas bad for her? I can't stand them; they're so ugly and loud. Not that I'm profiling. I just worry that they'll make her sick. What's the appeal and what should I do?

Yuck! Jacob, Northfield, IL

Dear Jacob,

There's a lot to unpack here, Jacob. First, your claim that Poolie eats more cicadas than any other dog.

You may be a Giant, sir, but how dare you! I've eaten nearly *all* the cicadas, so your bragging is like a gauntlet across my muzzle. Were you here and not Northfield, whatever that is, you'd leave me little recourse but to ask you and Poolie to step outside. Which is where I keep my cicadas.

To understand the appeal of cicadas, one must *think* like a cicada. That's easier for some dogs, like Brisby, my co-canine, who is far larger than these insects except for his ... well, I'd whisper the letters for "B-R-A-I-N" if I could spell.

Like terriers, cicadas live for the hunt. Oddly, they seem to prefer being the prey. Why else would they choose to be slow and clumsy and noisy and delicious?

Brisby, who I love like a littermate, couldn't care less about the etiquette of hunting. During cicada season, he frolics around our backyard like a fat Giant at a wedding reception that he's not paying for. He feasts with abandon, snatching bugs newly emerged from their burrows before they have time to say, "That's it? That's my life?"

Cicada and dog wage titanic battle while far below,
a city looks on with casual disinterest.

Brisby is a soldier without honor. A warrior without a code. On the plus side, he misses a lot of cicadas that I get.

So, to your question, Jacob, is it safe to eat cicadas? Obviously not for the cicadas. And that, I put squarely on *their* shoulders. If they have shoulders. Never really taken the time to look.

Are cicadas toxic to canines? Most dogs would answer, "I'll let you know. Can I go out now?" However, my Yelly Giant was watching a Nat Geo program on ecological stuff to worry about. A scientist said nothing about cicadas making dogs sick. And those scientists worry about *everything!* "Ooooo! I'm a scientist! Listen to me! Don't swim in shark-infested waters! Don't climb K2! Don't travel in outer space! You might get a tummy ache!"

Obviously, Jacob, eating cicadas shouldn't be a problem for Poolie. And if occasionally she overindulges, she can do what I do: throw up on the carpet. Then it's a problem for Giants.

Budleigh

NOT A BLACK HOLE
LOT OF EXCITEMENT FOR DOGS

Dear Budleigh,

I'm filled with awe and wonder that scientists have captured the first images ever of a supermassive black hole. Some describe it as the Eye of Sauron, others as a glowing one-way portal to Eternity. To me, it looks like my right eye in junior high after I took a line drive to the face.

Still, awe and wonder!

As the darkest entities in the universe, black holes are impossible to see, say astronomers. I totally understand their mathematical reasoning: An intense gravitational field that ... something, something. Einstein's theory ... something, something ... time and space. Really, really big ... something, something ... Star Trek.

Despite my excitement, Anka, my Shar Pei, shows no interest in black holes. I'm sure that she understands as I've explained their importance. ("Anka! Outer space ... something, something ... cookies!") But she just rests her head on my knees and seems bored. Well, not about the cookies.

How can I ignite her scientific curiosity since I'm running low on dog treats?

Sincerely, Miriam and Anka, science geek and disinterested dog, Atlanta, GA

Dear Miriam and Anka,

Which ones are Shar Peis? With the wrinkly faces, right? Maybe Anka's excited but you can't tell.

More likely, black holes bore her. They bore me and most dogs. Probably because we see them everywhere all the time.

That's going to annoy Science, but Science is always vexed about something. Look how Giant Scientists scribble on their chalkboards. So angry!

Thanks to their keen Canine senses, dogs know that black holes hide in the basement making creepy noises.

Black holes just aren't that mysterious. OK, they're a *little* mysterious. Like the washing machine. Also, a bit scary. Like the washing machine's dark, front-loading, heat producing companion. *That* thing gives me the willies!

The angry scientists brag that the black hole they photographed is some 55 million light years away. But it's only half that distance if you're on four legs. They also claim their photo reveals the all-consuming nature of a black hole – a singularity so voraciously hungry even light waves cannot escape.

Brisby, my co-dog, eats like that. His food *and* mine. And everything three feet above ground and lower. Yet, nobody scribbles angrily on a chalkboard about *him*.

While like Anka, I don't share your excitement, Miriam, I can tolerate it. These photographs confirm the theories of your Giant Einstein who apparently was smart as a Border Collie, although poor at herding. Still, the data gathered by more than 200 researchers and eight telescopes worldwide was significant enough for six simultaneous international news conferences carried on multiple television networks. Although not on Animal Planet.

So … kudos, I suppose.

Just don't expect Canine enthusiasm over news of a fuzzy, glowing, orange doughnut with a dark chocolate center. That's not going to excite dogs. Except Brisby. He's *so* hungry.

Budleigh

DOES ANYBODY REALLY KNOW WHAT TIME IT IS?

Dear Budleigh,

I read about a new study indicating that dogs may have an inner clock which would explain how Cinnamon, our Cocker Spaniel, always knows exactly when it's time for meals. However, here in Illinois, we just switched from daylight savings time ("Spring forward. Fall back!") and my little sweetie is annoyed that her food is being served late.

Is there a way to reset a dog's inner clock? Like a switch or button or something? I've scratched that adorable little patch of white on Cinnamon's muzzle. She loves that, but she's still running an hour ahead. An hour behind? Now I'm confused!

How can I adjust Cinnamon from daylight savings time?

Hoping for timely intervention, Claire S., Oak Park, IL

Dear Claire S.,

First, the correct term is daylight *saving* time. A Giant shouldn't need a Terrier to tell her that.

Next, the thought of having an inner clock makes my stomach a bit queasy. How'd it get there? I don't recall eating anything that keeps time. Except cicadas. And they're not very accurate.

Fortunately, a TV news story I overheard explained details of the study. My Yelly Giant further clarified by screaming, "Waste of taxpayers' money!" Simply put, research has uncovered a set of neurons in the medial entorhinal cortex of mouse brains that may play a role in encoding temporal aspects of episodic memories.

Well, *duh!* Did scientists even think to ask dogs? Dogs have learned a lot about mice. We don't just kill them for fun. Actually, it's a lot of fun. But they don't seem to tell time any better than cicadas.

Dogs' "Inner Clock" is easily confused by
the international date line.

The researchers, using slow, precise, boring methodologies that probably involved a lot of wires, now believe that mice can tell time. Further, this capacity may also hold for higher animals that have brains full of that medial blah-blah-blah, like cats, dogs and, in certain cases, Giants. That's why dogs seem to know when it's dinnertime.

There's an alternate theory known as "My Theory." Dogs stand around the kitchen at dinnertime because dogs always stand around the kitchen waiting for dinnertime. I mean, look at a dog's day: Sleep. Poop. *Dinner!* Our dance card isn't exactly full.

So, while you're off daylight *saving* time, Claire S., just feed Cinnamon an hour early. Then feed her again an hour later. Also feed me.

Oh, and about that reset button: When you scratch my belly, I thump my leg. Will that do?

Budleigh

BUDLEIGH GOES ALL SCATOLOG-ICK-AL!

Hey Budleigh!

Scientists in New Zealand have found a working USB memory stick filled with someone's vacation photos and videos frozen in a slab of leopard seal poop deposited on a beach.

I don't know what to do with this story, but I can't unread it.

Can you help sort it out?

Thanks! Closing My Eyes Just Makes It Worse, Boston, MA

Dear Closing,

While I sympathize with your trauma, as a dog I just can't relate. Giants are so reticent to discuss poop. Until they get old. Then that's *all* they talk about.

Not so with dogs. Poop is our CNN. It's how we stay informed. It's our primary topic of discussion, along with anything rodent related and the films of Woody Allen. (He's a genius!)

It's a mystery how a memory stick would end up in a leopard seal's poop. Also a mystery: What is a leopard seal? Is it a rodent? I'll bet it's a rodent!

My Giant Intern *Per Se* explains that a leopard seal, or *Hydrurga Leptonyx* (Latin for "I ate a what, now?") is Antarctica's second largest seal species with access to a laptop.

After removing the memory stick from the poop – or "scat" as scientists call it, which isn't much of an improvement – researchers carefully washed off all the good-smelling stuff. On the remarkably well-preserved drive they found the vacationers' photos of seal pups and a video shot from a kayak.

While wild animal "scat" can be revealing, some secrets dogs were not meant to know.

Unfortunately, there were no videos of the leopard seal "scatting" out the drive, which would have been interesting. But *Per Se* assures me *that* capability requires a far more advanced digestive system.

Still, imagine how cool!

Out of scientific curiosity and a supreme confidence that dogs are better than leopard seals, I brought this incident to the attention of the dog park, posing the question, "What have you 'scatted' of interest?"

LABRADOODLE: "Just recently, or …?"

CAVALIER KING CHARLES SPANIEL: "A paycheck. I don't know what that is or how it got there. Just don't do it! It freaks Giants."

BERNESE MOUNTAIN DOG: "Once, I scatted a mountaineer. He'd been missing for a week!"

DACHSHUND: "Really? A mountaineer? You're sure?"

BERNESE MOUNTAIN DOG: "Wait! Not scatted. Rescued!"

ROTTWEILER: "Ohhhh! See, that word 'scat' confused me, too. And I'm *huge!*"

MIXED BREED: "So 'scat' isn't a thing where they'd send me back to the shelter?"

DACHSHUND: "No, you're good."

MIXED BREED: "Cuz I'm not goin' back! Can't do it! Done my time!"

ROTTWEILER: "Easy, buddy! Listen, I've heard your Giant call you a Good Dog. They don't just say that. You're golden!"

MIXED BREED: "You're sure? Makes me so anxious! I ... I gotta get some air!"

DACHSHUND: "You're outside. There's *nothing* but air."

BERNESE MOUNTAIN DOG: "And scat!"

JACK RUSSELL TERRIER: "Yeah, about that. What's with leopard seals? Why's their scat getting them such publicity?"

All ponder. Mixed Breed hyperventilates.

LABRADOODLE: "Maybe Woody's casting them in a movie?"

JACK RUSSELL TERRIER: "Typical! Pushy, Hollywood rodents!"

Budleigh

BUDLEIGH TAKES
A WALK ON THE WILD SIDE

Hi Budleigh!

How worried should I be about my dog versus wild animals?

Our big backyard is right next to a forest preserve. Sometimes Nanook , our tough guy, zooms out the back door and charges all the way to the rear fence, barking wildly. The trees are pretty thick, so I can't tell what's there. But I've seen enough horror movies to suspect it's something terrible. Nanook returns when called, but he's not happy about it. I want him to be careful, but I don't want him doubting his manhood. Doghood. You know what I mean.

Thanks for your advice. Larry, Sheboygan, WI

Dear Larry,

OK, let's all stop ignoring the touchy issue of wild animals and squarely address what I call the "coyote in the dog park."

That is to say, "Oh m'God, there is a *Coyote* in the *Dog Park!*"

Recently I was walking my Giant through the neighborhood and was examining a particularly interesting pile of leaves when he shrieked like a chew toy, then yanked uncomfortably on our lifeline.

And just a quick word to Giants about the lifeline: Don't call it a "leash". That's offensive. It's like calling your dog a "mutt" instead of a "genetically diverse fur-enhanced co-worker."

Sorry, but it had to be said.

Anyway, my Giant yanks too hard, so I perform my fake choky sound, "Ah-HACK! Ah-HACK" that makes him feel guilty. But he only tightens his grip. I'm about to lodge a protest with his ankle when I spot the object of his concern: a proud coyote loping casually across the soccer field, regal of bearing, prideful of heritage.

Really makes one wonder. Where do you learn to *lope*?

Out of a sense of cross-species good will, I thought I'd follow him, maybe say "Hi," and share a pee. Instead, my Giant dragged me to the nearby gated dog park, shouting warnings to those inside that a coyote was loose, to be careful and watch their dogs!

I've never been so embarrassed.

Look, Larry, you Giants are worriers. But have faith that we dogs know how to choose our friends. We're not puppies anymore. Well, except for the puppies.

Admittedly, some animals are wilder than others. And a few tend to be a bit … slaughter-y. But dogs are cunning, canny, and remarkably resourceful. Remember, our species, *Canis Familiaris*, is Latin for "My harness has a pocket!" Scientists don't just make up those names!

I'm often invited to speak to wild animal herds, packs, and the occasional pod. Flattering, yes. But I'll cancel an event if I find the clearing strewn with piles of fresh, bloody bones. Or there's no bottled water. That's just common sense.

Highly perceptive dogs can sense
the subtlest clues of wildlife in their backyard.

Dogs are smart, brave, and proudly independent, Larry. So, trust that Nanook knows what he's doing and loosen your tight grip on that lifeline.

But don't let go! It's getting dark and kinda spooky out here. Also, you haven't given us dinner.

Budleigh

CLONING HAS BUDLEIGH
SEEING DOUBLE

Dear Budleigh,

So, Barbra Streisand cloned her dog? Seriously? They can do that? Does it cost a lot? How much lightning is involved? Is the clone exactly like the original dog or more of a sequel, like "Funny Lady" vs. "Funny Girl?" Could you explain the scientific process, the ethical and moral implications, and whether Barbra will headline the procedure? 'Cause I'm a big fan! So's Chip, who's a hound mix and very musical.

Thanks, Budleigh!

T.W. and Chip, Los Angeles

Dear T.W. and Chip,

It will come as no surprise to longtime readers that I have a very strong opinion on this issue, which is, "What's cloning?"

Usually when faced with a controversial topic I'm not familiar with, my Giants research it by watching MSNBC then yelling at each other until I find clarity. Since they were busy binge watching "The Crown," I explored the issue using SIRI. He's this Airedale I know from the dog park.

BUDLEIGH: "Hi SIRI! Hey, nice ball!"

SIRI: "Achh-ak ha-hauk unc!"

BUDLEIGH: "Sorry?"

SIRI: (*Drops ball.*) "I said, 'How can I help you?'"

BUDLEIGH: "What's a 'cloning?'"

SIRI: "Today will be warm and sunny. You have no appointments."

A biotechnology still in its infancy,
cloning can produce unexpected results.

BUDLEIGH: "Thanks! What about a 'Barbra Streisand?'"

SIRI: "Your destination is in 300 feet on the left!"

BUDLEIGH: "Great! So ... that's everything?"

SIRI: "Haunk-aug achh a'han!"

More recently I've learned that cloning is a process used to create DNA fragments, cells, or organisms and that Barbra Streisand has aged out of most movie roles.

Two of Barbra Streisand's dogs were cloned from her late dog Samantha, a Colon de Tulear. (*French for "Is this your colon?"*) Samantha was 14 years old, or about 98 in dog years. The cost was $50,000, or $350,000 in dog dollars.

While the cloning process is quite complicated, I'm sure I could perform it. Begin with a denucleated egg, then insert cultured somatic cells from the donor. Bake in a microwave-safe bowl for 30 minutes at 425 degrees. Let cool, then cut into identical dogs.

But is cloning right?

As a former shelter dog wrongly incarcerated with other homeless innocents, I should oppose cloning. I pulled myself up by my bootstraps, often chewing off those bootstraps. Every dog deserves that chance. But frankly, cloning's a *great* idea! Especially if *I* decide who's cloned.

Certainly, I'd clone one of my Giants – the yelly one who usually overfeeds me. Also that fat, black squirrel in the backyard. Just a little more practice and I *know* I can get him!

Obviously, I'd clone my tug-tug, food dish, and that particularly intriguing utility pole at the end of the street.

What else ... what else?

Oh, well *me*, of course! And by the thousands. Imagine great, majestic herds of me stretching to the horizon. What a gift to my Giants I would be. *We* would be.

But might such a sudden wealth of terriers cause my Giants to be overwhelmed, even dismayed?

Possibly. And ... *so*? If they need help, they can always ask SIRI.

Budleigh

WHAT IS "DOG"
BACKWARDS, AGAIN?

Hi, Budleigh.

I recently attended a Blessing of the Animals at a nearby church with my Basset, Grimace. My wife is Catholic, I was raised Jewish, my son says he's an atheist, and my daughter just insists she's for Bernie Sanders.

So what religion are dogs? Did we only confuse Grimace? He seemed to enjoy the service, except for a screeching parrot that scared him.

Appreciate your thoughts!

Best, Religiously Challenged, Omaha

Dear RC,

What religion are dogs? That's a question I get a lot.

I've been told – and firmly believe – that "dog" backwards is "god." I've also heard that "terrier" backwards is "god." Oh, and "cheese" backwards? Also "god."

I have faith that these are all true because I can't spell. Not even sure what "spell" is. But I do know this: parrots are nuts! And spooky!

Don't worry about Grimace. He seems spiritually grounded. I'm a bit concerned about your family, though.

Budleigh

Biblically and historically, dogs have played a significant theological role, especially at mealtimes.

Dogs and Children
– When Species Collide

Dear Budleigh,

Do you get along with kids? My toddler is infatuated with dogs. She won't go anywhere without her toy "Fooby." But somehow, she's detached both of Fooby's ears and split a seam where he once had a tail.

Could that behavior be a problem someday? How can I prepare her for a world full of Canines?

With thread in hand, Jan W.

Dear Jan W.,

Just so we're all on the same page, Fooby's a *stuffed* dog, right? And he's always been stuffed?

If so, it's not too late for your toddler to be rehabilitated.

Although unavoidable, mixing dogs and little Giants can be tricky. As Fooby learned to his sorrow, little Giants view dogs as a collection of removable parts in a Fisher-Price "My First Mammal" play set. Meanwhile, dogs appreciate little Giants as a renewable source of crumbs and spills. Such misunderstandings usually result in a child receiving a time out and a dog being wrapped in thick canvas restraints, then shoved into an unmarked van.

Of course, children need to be taught how to behave properly around dogs. But far be it from me to lecture Giants since they greatly outweigh me and are the source of my food supply.

Instead, let me offer advice to my many Canine readers ... well, not *readers* exactly ... about how to interact safely with little Giants so that *they* have a positive experience, and *you* avoid being shoved into an unmarked van.

Innocent, playful, and destructive,
children take an imaginative view of dogs.

1. Children are like puppies, only with access to lawyers.

When two Giants meet, they exchange business cards. When two dogs meet, they sniff behinds. A successful child-and-dog encounter will incorporate both, thus:

CANINE: "Why, hello, little Giant! Are you from the shelter?"

LITTLE GIANT: "Ak-Gooo! Ak-Gooo!"

CANINE: "Sorry, don't know that command. Are you saying, 'My hands are coated up to the shoulders in peanut butter'? If that is the case, please let me render assistance."

LITTLE GIANT: "Ek-Ek AK-GOOO!"

CANINE: "If by that you mean you're seeking a trash receptacle with the goal of ridding yourself of that indescribable smelly mass gripped between your fingers, please again allow me to alleviate that burden."

LITTLE GIANT: "Blaaarf!"

CANINE: "Oh, I'll clean that up! A pleasure doing business with you!"

2. Pay attention to body language, Nature's Instagram.

Pulling ears, twisting tails, and poking eyes are activities common among young children and the Trump administration. When encountering little Giants, carefully read their body language to know their intentions. Likewise, read the body language of Giant Parents, especially when they're screaming that they hate you.

Warning phrases include:

"Is that goddamn dog here?"

"I sleep with a loaded .38. Soooo …"

"Did you lock up that goddamn dog?"

"Why even have a dog? Shouldn't you have children by now?"

"Kill that goddamn dog!"

"What's that awful smell?"

"Goddamn dog!"

"… and they never found the body. Fact!"

3. Even us goddamn dogs need a little space.

Despite being slow on four feet, unsteady on two, and encumbered by too many probing fingers, little Giants can be great fun. Like us, they appreciate poop, own great squeaky toys, and howl for no apparent reason.

However, unlike us – and I know this sounds crazy – they don't *live* to nap.

Why would any animal – even a Giant – not want to nap? I've taken three naps just writing this column. To maintain peak performance, a dog needs to nap at least 24 hours a day.

Not so with little Giants. They shun their bed to run all morning in the park like squirrels (NOTE TO CANINES: They are *not* squirrels!), spend the afternoon digging holes in the garden like chipmunks (IMPORTANT! See previous note), then splash in the bath like fish (OK, fish aren't on our list.) Yet, they still have enough energy to roll Thomas the Train over your tail and up your back while you're napping.

Brrrr! That Thomas the Train really creeps me out! What's with the eyes?

Where then, dog readers, is it safe to nap away from a little Giant intent on playing Alien Autopsy on you? Obviously, it's wherever *they're* supposed to take a nap – their bed, or crib, or crate. Just curl up there. They'll never find you.

But if they do, stay calm, rest your head on their lap, and give them the sad Thomas the Train eyes. The child will be captivated, Giant Parents will be charmed, and you'll avoid being wrapped in canvas and shoved in a van.

Everyone's a winner!

Budleigh

Your Dog
or Your Boyfriend.
Is That Really a Question?

Dear Budleigh,

I came across your column while looking for advice about keeping New Year's resolutions. So, are you a dog or what? If you are, maybe you can help me with my Resolution No. 4: Train Shanda, my Samoyed, to like my boyfriend. Or maybe just not snap at him so much. He's a wonderful guy, but he's never had a dog, so he does things that upset Shanda. Like sitting in her chair. Or at the kitchen table. Or anywhere, really. Also, Shanda barks too much when he's around. But I think he startles her. He's very tall.

Any suggestions on how to bring these two together? I'd have them hug it out, but Daniel – that's the boyfriend – doesn't trust Shanda's teeth so close to his throat. But she's such a sweetie!

Best regards, Soon to be Single? Cleveland, Ohio

Dear Single,

Yes, I'm a dog. And while it's reasonable to ask my credentials, perhaps you're just avoiding the real question: What's a Samoyed?

I thought it a brand of athletic footwear, *per se*. However, I'm informed by *Per Se*, my intern, that a Samoyed is indeed a dog, just not one of the cute ones. Of course, that's both a matter of Giants' personal taste and their *per se*.

Establishing a bond between Canine and Giant Boyfriend is fraught with challenges, especially if dog is aggressive and Boyfriend is made of some tasty meat. But there are effective techniques for building rapport, provided Boyfriend respects Shanda as an equal, not just another brand of athletic footwear.

Credit dogs as infallible judges of character. Is it possible that your heart is ignoring Boyfriend's flaws that Shanda perceives? Boyfriend's admission that he'd never had a dog was revealing. Did you rightly ask, "Are you from Hell? Do you cast a reflection? Was "The Exorcist" funny?" His answers, though painful, might have spared you heartache as well as a curse of boils.

Dogs often perceive subtle flaws in your boyfriend that you've overlooked.

But let's say that Boyfriend is relatively human and, as you say, "a wonderful guy." So, what's he done for Shanda lately? In fact, what's he done for *me*? Much like a restaurant maître d' and all elected officials, distrustful dogs like bribes. Something as simple as a small biscuit can win a dog's friendship, until you run out. But does Boyfriend greet Shanda at the door with a pocketful of treats? Doubtful. Does he meet me with a pocketful of live field mice? Never! And you wonder I don't like the guy?

Date night offers another opportunity to foster Boyfriend's loving relationship with Shanda and, to a lesser extent, you. Include pup in activities usually reserved for you and Boyfriend – moonlight walks, dining al fresco, solving jigsaw puzzles — the ones with the big pieces because, ya know, paws.

However, even if Daniel insists, avoid involving Shanda in quasi-criminal actions, like pulling a bank job. Unlike Daniel, Canines are highly moral and law-abiding, although many make excellent wheelmen.

So, Single, is it time to kick Daniel to the curb while Shanda showers clods of dirt over him? That's your call. But if you believe he's a keeper despite Shanda's caution and my shrill, insistent warning howls, then make the effort to bring Canine and Giant Boyfriend together.

But be patient! Take baby steps. Especially if you're wearing that popular brand of athletic footwear.

Budleigh

BUDLEIGH REMINDS VACATIONERS, "HEY, YA GOT THIS DOG HERE!"

Dear Budleigh,

I'm really looking forward to a summer getaway, but am worried about Hanover, our mixed breed "guilt hound," who can't come with us. She was a shelter dog, so I worry about boarding her in case she suffers flashbacks. But what if I hire a pet sitter who, it turns out, is a Satanist looking for a sacrifice?

Whatever I do, Hanover's going to give me "the look" – Where do dogs learn that? – which says that somehow, I've let her down. Again! Maybe instead of traveling we should just stick with another stay-cation, and movie marathon-cation, and tub-of-Ben-&-Jerry's—cation.

Any advice would be appreciated.

Hoping to get the Hell out of Dodge, Janelle, Chicago

Dear Janelle,

Separation from their dogs can be a very emotional issue for Giants. The best approach is first to ask yourself, "Just how *many* Satanists live in the neighborhood?"

For me, I suspect two, those Giants who own the black dog with the pointy ears who pees – and I've witnessed this! – on my hydrangea shrubs. Tell me *that* isn't the act of Lucifer's hellhound.

Next, spare yourself anxiety over boarding or sitting Hanover. Dogs rarely pine away when their Giants leave. Five minutes after you walk out the door, we usually forget who you are. Tests conducted by scientists at a prestigious Giant university proved this. Seventy percent of dogs surveyed immediately forgot their owners. The other 30 percent forgot to show up for the test.

The point is we'll be fine without you, and eager to greet you as friendly strangers when you return. Meanwhile, here are a few tips to smooth the transition:

Wary dogs view a stay in a luxury kennel as just crate training at a Sandals Resort.

We're not stupid! We know what suitcases mean.

Look, Giants, cunning isn't your long suit. So don't waste time hiding suitcases in The Ever-closed Spare Room, then sneaking in piles of clothes. Dogs know when something's going on. Just like we know that "Who" wants to go for a "Ride" in the "Car?" means a visit to the Giant Vet to get something stuck in us.

Instead, be frank with your dog. Explain that you're going on a trip, probably won't return, so the pantry is his. He won't be upset because he'll forget in minutes.

What *exactly* do you mean by "kennel"?

Like most dogs, I've no problem being boarded at a kennel provided it's on my Giants' bed.

However, due to zoning restrictions, kennels are rarely so conveniently located. Some are quite far away, out in the country. Possibly near that farm where a heavily sedated Roxy the Boxer was taken after the unfortunate "playground incident." He must have enjoyed it there since he never returned.

Kennels vary widely in the amenities they offer. Giants should carefully research the facilities for the following before booking a cell:

- No bullwhips
- Convenient shopping, nightlife, a tree
- Onsite dining; can opener
- Netflix
- Stinky, smelly stuff; spa

Leave detailed care instructions on how to work my food bowl.

Preferable to a kennel is to hire an in-house dog sitter well known to your Canine and, ideally, bacon-flavored.

117

Yet, despite your best efforts to put in place a person so familiar that they know how to work your TV remote, the key to success is trust between sitter and dog:

GIANT SITTER: "Hey, girl! Who wants to go walkies? Do you want walkies? Who wants walkies?"

CANINE: "I assume you're licensed and professionally bonded?"

GIANT SITTER: "Oh, you're a shy girl!"

CANINE: "Let's just take it slow, OK? Now, you've credentials?"

GIANT SITTER: "We'll go play in the park! Where's your ball? Go get your ball!"

CANINE: "Ex-CUSE me! The ball does *not* go to the park. That's a rule put in place by ... by ... you know, that nice couple who left here a few minutes ago. I forget their names...."

GIANT SITTER: "C'mon, sweetie! I know you've gotta go."

CANINE: "I can hold it. Or pee in your slippers."

GIANT SITTER: "You can have treats —?

CANINE: "Not hungry."

GIANT SITTER: "And scratchies —"

CANINE: "Not itchy."

GIANT SITTER: "And Netflix!"

CANINE: "Hurry up! "Westworld" starts in an hour!"

Budleigh

DOGS ARE A BARGAIN!
EXCEPT FOR THE MONEY

Dear Budleigh,

I'm having a disagreement with my Cockapoo, Mighty, and I'm hoping you can straighten out one of us. Maybe both.

According to a recent Cost of Dog Ownership Survey conducted by the website Rover, people drastically underestimate the costs of owning a dog. Most believe a dog costs between $26 and $75 per month. When I stopped crying bitter tears, I read that dog owners spend an average $153 per month.

Mighty, who is 14 years old, considers that reasonable. I say he owes me $137,624. But I'll settle for $125K. Mighty insists that he's paid his way in licks and kisses and scaring away squirrels and invisible monsters. He raises a good point. Am I wrong to keep things on a strictly cash basis?

Hope you can settle this while I'm out walking Mighty.

Best, Sam and Mighty the Cockapoo, Illinois

Dear Sam and Mighty,

To be honest, Giant money confuses me. What is it, one dollar equals seven dog years or something like that? I have a Giant Intern to deal with all that.

As a Terrier, I analyze a lot of scientific surveys. Some produce useful data; others, dubious results best described as the kind of stuff I deposit twice a day on our neighbor's lawn. But most often, surveys generate more questions than answers.

This Rover survey begs the question: Who still names their dog "Rover"? That's like from the Columbian Exposition, right? Are they being ironic? Dogs don't appreciate irony. Too much to explain at the dog park.

As "Mighty" must know.

Budgeting for your dogs' needs can be expensive. Especially, if they're collectors of fine art.

The survey breaks down the true cost of owning a dog into four categories: One-time expenses, monthly costs, annual costs, and potential expenses.

This is very similar to how I rate my Giants: "What have you done for me?"; "What have you done for me *lately?*"; "Have you thought about what you can do next?"; and "I'm hungry!"

One-time costs can run as high as $1,487, according to the survey, and include such expenses as adoption fees; flea, tick, and heartworm medications; crate and bed; "pee pads" and poop bags.

Monthly costs include food, toys, treats and poop bags. Potential expenses can take in emergency vet bills, dog training (Hahahaha! *Good* one!), grooming, and, I assume, poop bags.

To the untrained eye, poop bags seem to be the problem. But let's hang on to those "pee pads," shall we? I don't know what they are, but they sound interesting.

To your question, Sam, where can expenses be reduced that's fair to Giants while not taking advantage of a dog's inability to reason?

I've struggled with this because of my inability to reason. However, the survey also found that for the sake of their dogs, a good percentage of Giants would give up alcohol, takeout/food delivery, and coffee.

Fine! Do that!

Also, a third of Giants surveyed would throw a birthday party for their dog, nearly half would take their dog out for a special birthday meal, and a quarter have paid for a massage for their dog.

Sam, do you get the sense that maybe, just maybe you still *owe* Mighty?

And Mighty, that tennis ball rolls both ways. What are you willing to give up for Sam?

I suggest poop bags.

Budleigh

Budleigh Offers
Food for Thought

Dear Budleigh,

So, what is the best dog food? I feed Roscoe, my Beagle, a nutritious mixture of dry and canned food that the vet recommended. Roscoe seems satisfied since he eats it all in four seconds. And he's healthy. But I wonder if he's really enjoying his meals? I'd really appreciate an average dog's perspective.

No offense.

Thanks!

Jacob of #Jacob&Roscoe

Dear Jacob, Roscoe and Hashtag,

On advice of counsel, I've been told not to recommend specific brands of dog food until such time as they pay my Giant.

However, since I'm a Terrier, rules don't apply to me. So, I'm not afraid to name names. The best-tasting, most nutritious and economical dry food for Roscoe comes in that big bag with a picture of a dog on it.

It's also available in a smaller bag that features a picture of a dog. Only a smaller dog.

There! *Now* I've done it. Let the lawsuits begin!

Among Giants nowadays, "nutritious" seems to be *the* popular buzz word, just slightly ahead of "redacted" and "impeachment." But as you smartly point out, Jacob, dogs appreciate food that's good tasting, even if it's not nutritious. Even if it's unhealthy. Even if it's a loaf of cornbread. Left on the kitchen table. Uncovered.

Budleigh solves the dilemma of "healthy" versus "good tasting" by eating whatever's closest.

Sorry! Drifted off there for a moment.

What is "good tasting" varies among dogs. For example, I have a fairly refined palate that includes everything my Giants toss in the big bin under the sink, access to which is restricted due to national security concerns.

My dog park friend Roxy the Boxer, however, insisted that food tastes best when you've run it down, torn its throat, and savored the taste of hot, fresh blood in your jaws. He said that a lot. In fact, that's all Roxy ever talked about until he was captured, forced into a van and, I've heard, taken away to a farm where he could run and run, never to be seen again.

My point is: Chicken! If Roscoe is like me – and I'm certain he wants to be – he'll really enjoy a dog food with chicken. I'm not sure what chicken is, but it also comes in cans. And maybe in corn bread.

To assure dog food quality, always check the ingredients. They should break down as follows:

50% – Chicken, fish, beef, lamb, stuff from the bin under the sink

50% – Goes to Budleigh

50% – Grains (That is, if cornbread is a grain)

50% – Prey (Increase this percentage for Roxy the Boxer)

50% – That grey stuff the gardener spreads on the gladiolas

50% – Cicadas

50% – That stuff on my right hind foot

50% – Goose poop

50% – That stuff on *another* dog's right hind foot

If this math is confusing, Jacob, ask Roscoe to explain. I wouldn't expect an average Giant to understand.

No offense.

Budleigh

HERO OR HUNGRY?

Dear Budleigh,

Did you see that video on social media where a Golden Retriever called Storm drags a drowning baby deer from the ocean? Then Storm nuzzles and paws it, and probably would have attached a defibrillator if he was vocally able to shout, "Clear!" Dogs are awesome! Do you think I can train Millie, my Rat Terrier, to be that cool or has that ship sailed?

Love your column! Michael M., Madison, WI

Dear Michael M.,

I've heard about Storm's dramatic rescue, but not seen it because I can't access social media due to paws.

However, my Giants seemed quite taken with the story, watching it repeated on the news shows, praising Storm with teary eyes, then sighing at me.

OK, Giants, message received!

Why is anyone surprised that a dog would save an animal? Dogs do that all the time, especially showboats like Goldens. What's praiseworthy is when we save animals even when we're kinda hungry.

Rescue or kill animals? Frankly, I don't see the difference, but I'm thinking Big Picture. I've rescued a number of rabbits, but just for a couple of minutes. Whether my intention was to save or kill them, we were all just having a bit of fun.

Not them, of course.

Budleigh attempts to "rescue" a wild tiger and return it to the jungle – with mixed results.

The Giant Vet called me a "natural predator," which I thought was rude to say right in front of my Giants. They're worriers, although they appreciate a vegetable garden free of vermin.

So, is Rat Terrier Millie more savior or killer? Her breed's name would indicate deep inner conflicts. To help resolve such cases I developed this simple diagnostic chart; The Great Chain of Eating. Score one point for every animal Millie would kill and one for each she'd befriend. Then add a bunch of extra points, if you'd like. I don't know what to do after that.

Animal	Characteristics
Flies	Small. Buzzy. Helpless. Tasty. (Not the green ones!)
Cicadas	Large. Clumsy. Often entangled in fences. Sad and delicious.
Butterflies	Don't bother chasing. These things know a trick.
Birds	See Butterflies.
Larger things	Squirrels. Chipmunks. Mice. They're all the same, right? Just different costumes?
Dogs	Do *not* kill! Bad manners, terrible PR.
Creatures that fight back	Includes anything with claws, spines, fangs, sharp edges or broken glass. Save or kill at your discretion.
Humans	Which ones?

Please share these tips with Millie, Michael M. It might help her fulfill her lifesaving, heroic potential. Or barring that, just fulfill her hungry tummy.

Budleigh

The Latest Dirt
on Dog Germs

Dear Budleigh,

Should I be worried about germs tracked in by my dirty dog? A recent story in the New York Times cites research that dogs bring an array of micro-organisms into our overly scrubbed homes that might actually be salutary to helping us stave off a number of illnesses by strengthening our autoimmune system. If true, our Newfoundland, Greta, will be much relieved! She worries so.

Thanks for your thoughts. Ingrid G.

Dear Ingrid G.,

"Salutary"? Don't know that word, but if it means "with meat sauce," then I agree!

My Giants are avid readers of the New York Times, and, of course, as a puppy I often peed on it. So, I'm well familiar with the high journalistic quality and absorbency of that paper's content. And their story spotlights a major controversy: should a travel ban be placed on micro-organisms seeking to enter our homes.

As I understand it from my Yelly Giant, immigration across our threshold is restricted for micro-orgs from several regions. Those vicinities are:

- The dirt pile I dug by the garden trellis
- The dirt pile I dug by the roof downspout
- The dirt pile I dug between the trellis and the downspout
- Iran
- Where I killed that bunny
- Where I killed that other bunny
- Where they suspect a chipmunk was killed, but nothing was ever proved.

Some dogs track in dirt inadvertently.
Others make it their career objective.

While Giants often complain about germs, I welcome them. Especially the ones with meat sauce. For germs, which are just micro-orgs without any formal education, life is hard, jobs are scarce, and poop is limited.

As a formerly homeless Terrier, I too knew hardship until my Giants took me in and learned to cater to my every whim. That's why I sponsor so much dirt in my house. Clinging to it are teeming multitudes of germs yearning to benefit me and do what I want.

Thus, it is the duty of Canines to raise up our germs to stand proudly upon our shoulders. If Canines had shoulders, rather than withers. And if germs had legs, rather than chromosomes.

Equally, it is the responsibility of Giants to support all policies of their Canines, from "Soap Is Tyranny!" to "What'd'ya Mean This Is *Your* House?" That last is critically important, as Giants tend to reduce dogs to second-class citizens or worse, pets!

So, fellow Canines, remind your Giants that the leash pulls both ways! Howl with me that classic Woody Guthrie song of unity, glory, and training treats:

"This land is YOUR LAAAAAND, This land is MY LAAAAAND

Well, mostly *MY* LAAAAAND, I suppose some's YOUUUUR LAAAAAND!

You can have the BAAAAASEMENT. Or the upstairs BATHTUUUUB!

Everyyy-where else belongs to MEEEEEE!!!"

Budleigh

WINNIN' AND WAGGIN'!

Hiya Budleigh!

How about them Cubs? Do you think you'd like to be their new mascot?

Yay Cubs! Yay Budleigh!

Donna, Buffalo Grove

Dear Donna,

My Giants would like that. They've been waiting to win a championship for 756 dog years.

Me? I'm not sure. I'm good at chasing balls. Just not so much at giving them back.

Is that gonna be a problem?

Budleigh

Budleigh and his Giants attend
Furry Fan Forehead Day at Wrigley Field

THE GIANT AS EMOTICON

Dear Budleigh:

I'm really asking this question on behalf of my Giants. It must be really important, because they ask me ALL THE TIME!!!!

"Who's a good dog?"

Best, Leia the Beagle

Dear Leia,

Careful here, dear! Because Giants are so adorable, it's easy to forget that they're only capable of the most basic feelings and emotions like joy, fear, and overdrawn.

Giants that excitedly ask, "Who's a good dog?", especially while repeatedly slapping their thighs and comically widening their eyes, are revealing more about themselves than about you. "Who's a good dog" is simply a reliable indicator of your Giant's good health, especially when their nose is moist and their coat glossy and lustrous.

Conversely, when your Giant storms into the room, hands on hips, and asks, "Did you do this? DID YOU DO THIS?", clearly, they're telling you that they aren't feeling well, maybe from eating grass. I mean, that *can't* be a sincere question. Did *I* do it? Of *course* I did it! Who else is here? Brisby? Nature's

Perfect Animal? He never does *anything*, does he? Honestly, I think he's stuffed. And I say that with love.

Look, Leia, understanding your Giant's behavior isn't rocket science. Probably. I don't know what "rocket" is. Or "science." But what I do know, as I so often remind readers, is that I'm a Terrier. So, I know more than everybody.

Brisby, Nature's Perfect Animal,
training to fit in by doing nothing.

Here's a checklist of common Giant behaviors and their meaning. Hope that this helps.

GIANT BEHAVIOR:

"Do you want to go for a walk? Should we go for a walk? Let's go for a walk!"

MEANING:

I love bagging poop!

GIANT BEHAVIOR:

(*Clutches treat to chest.*) "Sit!"

MEANING:

Debase yourself for scraps.

GIANT BEHAVIOR:

"You're a smart dog! Such a smart dog!"

MEANING:

You're a Terrier. Probably Budleigh.

GIANT BEHAVIOR:

"Oh, you're filthy! Somebody needs a bath!"

MEANING:

Brisby needs a bath.

GIANT BEHAVIOR:

"Get off my bed!"

MEANING:

"Get off what I once thought of as my bed!"

Remember, Leia, you've more control than you think. Next time your Giant whines, "*Who's a Good Dog?*", stand firm and respond, "Aren't 'good' and 'bad' mere artificial constructs of a value system molded of established morals, norms or goals preexisting within a Society, epistemologically speaking?"

Unless they're holding a cookie. Then, just sit. Maybe bark.

Budleigh

Washing Machines
of Mass Destruction

Oh Great Dr. Budleigh,

My sweet Golden Retriever heard the sounds of an unbalanced washing machine (loud banging) and the fearless Lily is shaking and quaking at the thought of entering that hallway. I've tried a trail of treats, a heap of food, and nothing has cured her. She eats her meals close to said washing machine, now dubbed the Great and Powerful Oz, so any thoughts on a cure?

Eternally grateful to ya! Lisa H.

Dear Lisa,

To be clear, I'm not a doctor, although I *do* have a license. Also a microchip in my neck.

However, I often counsel fearful dogs – usually while cowering under the bed with them – to help them face their issues, confront their anxieties, and, ideally, share those trails of treats you mentioned.

It's not surprising that a dog would be frightened by a washing machine that's unbalanced, and from your description, possibly psychotic. It's just that Lily's a Golden Retriever, so society expects more from her.

Canines have feared washing machines since Homo Sapiens first climbed down from the trees to put in a load of soiled linens. Frankly, we've always marveled why you Giants *aren't* afraid of them. Washing machines hum and vibrate and make scary, thumpy sounds. They swallow clothes whole, then spit them up drenched, cold, and probably angry. And sometimes, bubbly, white foam erupts from their mouths. Kind of like Roxy the Boxer's mouth before he was dragged from the dog park and shipped to a nice, big farm in the country. We're told.

And you're *not* scared? Wake up, Giants!

A dedicated counselor must be willing to venture far afield. Even under the bed.

The best way to treat Lily's fears is through desensitization, a 12-step program that dogs can complete in a third of that because of all their legs.

For starters, acclimate Lily to the washing machine by bringing them together in a safe, neutral space. Try letting them sleep together in your bed. Or carry the washing machine when you take walks.

Next, if trails of treats have failed to entice Lily, consider filling the entire washing machine with her dog food. True, this might be harsh on your laundry, but today's stain-resistant fabrics are surprisingly hardy.

And what's with all that clothes washing anyway? Are Giants really that dirty? Don't bother washing up for us. Dogs enjoy their Giants' odor. I'm sure Lily loves how you stink, Lisa. We all do. Probably.

Look, Lisa, you're clearly a good Giant devoted to Lily's well-being. That's why I recommend that you both enroll in my complete 12-step fear-desensitization program, which is tax deductible and chicken-flavored.

Of course, your washing machine also is welcome to attend, although without feet, completing those 12 steps will take *forever.*

Budleigh

THE VETERINARIAN IS IN!
BUDLEIGH OFFERS ADVICE ON
NOT SWALLOWING PILLS

Dear Budleigh,

Daisy, my Labradoodle, has a skin rash and she has to take pills. She really hates that and tries to spit them out. Also, she tries to hide under things that are way too small for her, like an antique end table.

I don't want her to be so anxious. Could you, maybe, talk to her?

Thank you! Carla H., Seattle, Washington

Dear Carla,

Labradoodle? Really? That's a thing now? OK, no judgments.

Much of the blame for Daisy's – and all dogs' – reluctance to swallow pills can be laid at the feet of Giant Veterinarians who routinely treat illnesses with medicines rather than exploring alternative cures, like bacon.

I may have had no formal education beyond Basic Obedience and Leash Etiquette, (instructor's critique: "Budleigh pulls. May not be college material.") but if bacon is "cured" and an illness needs a "cure," well, you do the math, since I can't.

So, we're stuck with pills.

However, although I sympathize with your request that I talk directly with Daisy, that would erode the trust of my readers. Plus, her skin rash? Ewwww! Let's just keep this as girl talk between me and you. Except I'm a boy. Oh, and a dog.

A dog's anxiety to take pills is often directly related to their Giant's anxiety over losing fingers. They need to meet somewhere in the middle, but no lower than the wrist.

**Budleigh demonstrates how to reject a pill
with extreme prejudice.**

You, the Giant, should first offer the pill to her, the dog, to determine if she's interested. That should give you both a good laugh, which will lower the tension.

Next, try coating the pill in something smelly and delicious. Like a muddy leather boot or, more economical, peanut butter. Peanut butter is why dogs *know* there's a God. I would eat a pill slathered in peanut butter. I'd eat a hissing, crunchy bug slathered in peanut butter. Well, honestly, I'd eat the hissing, crunchy bug anyway, but I'd enjoy some peanut butter after.

But I've heard Giants complain that peanut butter is messy and quite difficult to coat pills, let alone frantically hissing, crunchy bugs. So, let's consider an alternate drug delivery system known as, "Those soft, chewy treats with the pill hidden inside that I can spit out™."

As the name implies, there's a drawback. So, the next tactic is to mix the pill into the morning or evening meal. This satisfies Giants, who can observe food and medication consumed, and dogs, who then spit out the pill at their leisure.

As is often the case with Giants, you can always stoop to brute force by prying open a dog's jaws, shoving a pill deep in its mouth using your dirty fingers that smell vaguely of muddy, leather boot, then stroking their throat until they swallow – an interrogation technique refined during the Cold War.

The best tactic of all, though, is to take advantage of that unique trust between Canine and Giant that has evolved over 30,000 years. Or 210,000 in *our* years. You Giants trust us to guard, protect, and defend. We trust you to turn doorknobs.

Carla, I recommend that you sit down with Daisy and calmly explain the situation. Point out her skin rash, (Ewwww!) show her the pill, let her sniff and lick it, then in the spirit of trust, swallow it yourself. I guarantee that a teary-eyed and grateful Daisy will eagerly swallow the next one.

And if not, well, no offense, it might improve your skin.

Budleigh

EXTOLLING CONSOLING

Dear Budleigh,

When is it appropriate to get another dog?

Our sweet Izzy crossed the Rainbow Bridge six months ago. Bitzy, her sister, has adjusted pretty well, we think. Except now in the middle of the night she jumps off the bed and checks all the rooms like a night watchman. I worry that's kind of obsessive behavior. But then, so is my following her around at night.

Nothing can replace our Izzy! But all of us, including Bitzy, miss the company of another dog. The question is, are we ready?

Izzy's family in Michigan City, MI

Dear Izzy's family,

I so sympathize with your loss of Izzy, whether over the Rainbow Bridge or in one of the rooms of your home.

Last year we lost Brisby, our Senior-level Administrative Canine. As he was a Very Good Boy, he too traveled the Rainbow Bridge, according to my Giants. After weeks of tears, they seemed to find tranquility sharing that beautiful rainbow image. Although to us Canines, such a bridge would be perceived in various shades of gray.

A lovely metaphor, though. I hope it's true. Brisby would have liked that. He enjoyed his walks and I'll bet a rainbow smells great!

So, how long before a new Canine should be inducted into your pack? For us, a year passed. Then came Cheadle.

A puppy of questionable ancestry, though probably a least one dog was involved, Cheadle came to us from an out-of-state home for strays. You know those kindly, no-kill animal shelters so popular nowadays? Well, this ain't one of 'em.

**"Someday, Cheadle, all this will be yours.
But right now, it's *mine!*"**

My Giants were told by the rescue agency that this four-month-old Labrador/Terrier mix had been sentenced to his own Rainbow Bridge, so they made room for him on the transport. Back then, he was referred to as "Ringmaster." My Giants named him "Cheadle." I call him "Green Mile."

Among the many, many confusions between Giants and Canines is that the former doesn't think the latter capable of feelings. In fact, Canines, like Giants, understand feelings better than they do the difference between "former" and "latter." Thus, when considering the addition of a new dog, it is imperative to include your current pets in the family discussion.

GIANT 1: "Hon, are we really ready for Cheadle?"

GIANT 2: "I am, Dave! It's time. We all miss our Brisby. Don't we, Budleigh? Yes, we do! Oh, yes, we do!"

BUDLEIGH: "Brisby's the grey one, right? Sleeps in the red wingback chair? Is the 'Good Dog?' Sure, I miss it. Him."

GIANT 2: "Actually, Budleigh's handled the loss of his Brisby pretty well, Dave. He was depressed for a while. But he seems OK now."

GIANT 1: "Dogs don't understand death."

BUDLEIGH: "Uh, *excuse* me? Have you talked with the rabbits out back? No! 'Cause there *aren't* any! Me and Brisby are two of their Four Horsemen!"

GIANT 1: "It's just that a new dog – and a puppy? That's a big step, hon!"

GIANT 2: "I know, Dave. Still, you know that we'll love him —"

BUDLEIGH: "But *less* than me, right?"

GIANT 2: "— and he'll keep Budleigh from getting bored."

BUDLEIGH: "I'm good! I've got the Internet! I stole your passwords."

GIANT 1: "How about just buying new toys for Budleigh —"

BUDLEIGH: "With squeakers!"

GIANT 1: "— or an obedience class?"

BUDLEIGH: "Hard pass!"

GIANT 1: "And what if they never get along?"

BUDLEIGH: "Hey, I got used to you two."

GIANT 2: "I don't have the answers, Dave. I just know that Brisby's loss left a dog-shaped hole in my heart."

GIANT 1: "And mine. I miss him so much. I still see him lying in the red wingback, guarding the neighborhood."

GIANT 2: "Nothing can ever replace Brisby, Dave. But he'd want us happy. He'd want a dog to have a home. He'd want us to love Cheadle. It might even help Budleigh process his grief and move on."

GIANT 1: "Yes! Let's do this!"

BUDLEIGH: "Just keep this Cheadle off the red wingback. Or Brisby's gonna be *really* pissed when he gets back!"

Budleigh

THE DOGS STRIP

(NOT AS DIRTY AS IT SOUNDS!)

Budleigh vs Godzilla vs Chance the Snapper

Gamesmanship...uh, Games-DOG-ship

Social, Yes. Distancing, Not So Much.

Godzilla vs Kong vs Budleigh

Tough Times!
And Tougher for Some

Piece on Earth

EpiDogue

Stop reading.

If at any point in this book you got a laugh, a chuckle, a smile, or even a persistent facial tic that you interpreted as a pre sneeze, then Budleigh's work here is done.

So, put down this book. Cuz, ya know, now it gets sad.

Through the midsummer of 2022, with Sleeping between Giants, Book II written, and torpid cicadas lounging about the backyard like juicy Tootsie Rolls begging to be eaten, Budleigh grew sluggish, then increasingly dull-eyed.

Stop reading.

Long story short – and it was mercifully short – Budleigh had developed cancer of the everything, as well as other problems. There was nothing to be done. He wasn't in pain, but that was inevitable. Until then, we kept him comfortable and close.

Within a month, and with the loving help of Countryside Animal Clinic, we sent our Budleigh across the Rainbow Bridge. I'm confident he was greeted by Brisby, excited to tell him how great everything there smells and how many hydrants there are!

If there are passed pups in your life, I'm sure that they, too, welcomed Budleigh — maybe helped show the new kid the ropes.

For our pack, life goes on. Just not quite as brightly. Cheadle, the new guy that Budleigh had hoped to corrupt, moped about for several days, occasionally checking under our bed that had been Budleigh's subterranean kingdom. Then, he simply accepted that there would be only one dog dish now, and that the red wingback chair in the living room remained Budleigh's, per Brisby's last will and testament.

Our family and friends were heartbroken and relieved. Budleigh – *never* Bud; *always* Budleigh – was a Good Dog, although he'd fancied himself as "edgy."

For me, Budleigh was my little muse; for him, I was a source of treats. And the occasional recipient of bites, if I tried to brush his fur without first submitting the proper paperwork.

More than anything, he was my Canine; I was his Giant.

Funny. Turns out he was my Giant, too.

Dave Jaffe, September 2022

ACKNOWLEDGMENTS

There's more to raising a dog than sticking food in one end, then cleaning up what comes out the other.

The same is true for writing a book, although sometimes the outcomes are similar.

The making of this book required the encouragement of a diverse cadre of dog lovers and author supporters.

Thanks to Konstantinos and Laura Louvros of Eggspresso restaurant and their wonderful staff, come and gone, for endless mugs of coffee and friendship.

Likewise, thanks to Drs. Michael Malitz and Richard Guelzow, and staff, including Mary Fierstein, Mary K., Chris Rivera, Naomi Levi, Robin Gutmann, and many others at Countryside Animal Clinic. They cared for and loved each of my dogs, from gangly puppyhood until that sad time we'd walk them, hand in paw, to the edge of Rainbow Bridge.

To copy editors Carleen Tibbetts and Pam Baert, whose laser-focused scrutiny of grammar, spelling, and punctuation had me constantly and defensively saying, "Oh yeah! I *knew* that. I just … forgot!"

And an h/t to dearest friends Emil and Donna Donoval who suggested the term, "Epidogue" at a time when this humorist needed to laugh.

Finally, to the many SbG blog readers who followed, commented, wrote in, shared stories, and encouraged this tired, old author: You are forever part of our pack.

Stay frisky!

HAVEN'T HAD ENOUGH OF BUDLEIGH? TRY LIVING WITH HIM!

Before SbG Book 2, there was SbG Book 1.

I mean, c'mon! That's just basic math!

Before Budleigh the Terrier knew everything, he was just a young, shelter dog who knew *everything*. Rescued by author Dave Jaffe and his wife because no one else seemed willing, this wily, intelligent, and fleetingly thoughtful, black-and-white Canine was proof of those old adages, "Smart as a terrier" and "Did he break the skin?"

Winner of the *2021 International Book Awards for Humor* and the *Indies Today 2019 Best Humor Book Award*, **Sleeping between Giants, Book 1: Budleigh, the Early Year** explores the highly successful, though often confusing relationship between Canines and Giants through essays, cartoons, and comic strips created by the author and drawn from his award-winning blog.

Our dogs know more than we think. And less than *they* think.

Order your copy on Amazon, and through your local booksellers.

Praise for
Sleeping between Giants,
Book I

"Dave Jaffe's obvious love for animals is matched by his talent for writing. Sleeping between Giants will make you laugh out loud with the author's Seinfeldian observations on life with a terrier."

Indies Today, 2019 **Best Book Award Winner for Humor**

"Any writer who can imagine a dog using the word 'fetlock' in a conversation is a winner in my book."

Judges remarks, **National Society of Newspaper Columnists**

"If you've ever wondered what your dog would say if he could talk — and if he had a fabulous sense of humor — this is the book for you. Sleeping between Giants is a laugh-out-loud funny dog's eye view of life. My favorite parts are the dialogs between the various dogs at the dog park, but basically there's something to snicker about on every page. Light and funny and entertaining, Sleeping Between Giants would make a perfect gift for anybody who has adopted — or is thinking about adopting — a shelter dog. (But I've got two pure bred Bichons in my life and I found it hilarious.)

Roz Warren, **author of "Our Bodies, Our Shelves: A Collection of Library Humor" and "Just Another Day at Your Local Public Library"**

"She's a very satisfied customer—I've never seen her so excited about a book!"

Submitted for Vex, **the chocolate Labrador of Giants Jess and Alex**